The Bhagavad Gita:
An Introduction

QUEST BOOKS

are published by
The Theosophical Society in America,
a branch of a world organization
dedicated to the promotion of brotherhood and
the encouragement of the study of religion,
philosophy, and science, to the end that man may
better understand himself and his place in
the universe. The Society stands for complete
freedom of individual search and belief.
In the Theosophical Classics Series
well-known occult works are made
available in popular editions.

Cover art: Stone sculpture outside the Vishnu temple at Kancipuram. Krishna talks to Arjuna while the armies line up before the battle of Kurukshetra.

Cover design by JANE EVANS

THE BHAGAVAD GITA

Its Philosophy and Cultural Setting

George Feuerstein

This publication made possible with the assistance of the Kern Foundation

The Theosophical Publishing House
Wheaton, Ill. U.S.A.
Madras, India / London, England

First Quest edition, 1983.

Library of Congress Cataloging in Publication Data

Feuerstein, Georg
The Bhagavad gita.

Originally published: Introduction to the Bhagavad-gita.
London: Rider, 1974.
Bibliography: p.
Includes index.
1. Bhagavadgita—Criticism, interpretation, etc.
I. Title
BL1138.66.F48 1983 294.5'924 82-42702
ISBN 0-8356-0575-2 (pbk.)

Printed in the United States of America

CONTENTS

NOTES TO TEXT, APPENDICES, SELECT BIBLIOGRAPHY, INDEX

In one salutation to thee, my God, let all my senses spread out and touch this world at thy feet.

Like a rain-cloud of July hung low with its burden of unshed showers let all my mind bend down at thy door in one salutation to thee.

Let all my songs gather together their diverse strains into a single current and flow to a sea of silence in one salutation to thee.

Like a flock of homesick cranes flying night and day back to their mountain nests let all my life take its voyage to its eternal home in one salutation to thee.

Rabindranath Tagore, *Gitanjali*, ciii.

ACKNOWLEDGEMENTS

I wish to thank the authors and publishers for permission to quote from the following works:

Collected Poems and Plays of Rabindranath Tagore, Macmillan, London. P. J. Saher, *Eastern Wisdom and Western Thought*, Allen & Unwin, London. S. Radhakrishnan, *Indian Philosophy*, volume I, Allen & Unwin, London. S. Radhakrishnan, *The Bhagavad-Gītā*, Allen & Unwin, London. S. Radhakrishnan, *The Brahma-Sūtra*, Allen & Unwin, London. [Śrī] Aurobindo, *Essays on the Gita*, Sri Aurobindo Library, New York. [Śrī] Aurobindo, *The Foundation of Indian Culture*, Sri Aurobindo Library, New York. K. N. Upadhyaya, *Early Buddhism and the Bhagavadgītā*, Banarsidass, Delhi. S. N. Dasgupta, *A History of Indian Philosophy*, volumes I and II, Cambridge University Press, Cambridge. Nataraja Guru, *The Bhagavad Gita*, Asia Publishing House, London. R. C. Zaehner, *The Bhagavad Gītā*, Clarendon Press, Oxford. A. W. Watts, *Psychotherapy East and West*, Pantheon Books, New York. G. Heard, *Pain, Sex and Time*, Cassell, London.

PREFACE

It has become almost banal to talk about the profound upheavals which Western culture now apparently undergoes. However, this should not blind us to the genuine hazards inherent in the present situation of mankind. The reasons for the fundamental cultural changes which we witness today are as varied and complex as they are difficult to comprehend. Perhaps the most prodigious and encouraging component of this overall turmoil is the revival of a genuine religious or spiritual need and appreciation, particularly among the young.

The ant-heap behaviour of modern human society, with its soul-destroying mechanical routine and organised aggression and violence, is only one of the negative aspects of the present crisis. There is another, intrinsically wholesome side to it: contemporary man is engaged in shattering the many gods, images and idols with which he has surrounded himself in the long course of history. And this process of maturation and emancipation is about to reach its most decisive phase, if it has not already done so. Man has become, if not more self-reliant, at least definitely more aware of his dependence—and, significantly enough, he has developed much greater *openness*.

Thorough discontentment with the inherited Western—Christian—tradition, especially with the 'God out there' dogma, has kindled a large-scale authentic search for truth in the 'heathen world', above all the spiritual heritage of the East. As was to be expected after the disappointment with Christian Theism, it is more the monistic schools, like Zen and Advaita-Vedānta, which captivate the interest of the disillusioned Westerner.

However, the immense appeal of these systems does not lie

exclusively in their metaphysical and theological standpoint or even their overall anti-intellectualism; what appears to be of far greater fascination is their experimental and autocratic approach: If you rigidly follow the prescribed rules, the predicted results will inevitably be achieved. There is no outside intervention, no need to depend on any indefinable agency. Everything has to be done by each person himself. Man is given full responsibility for all his actions, failures and successes.

In a sense, Monism justifies the emotional discord apparent in most of its Occidental followers and rationalises their self-centredness. This one-sided approach to the Eastern spiritual tradition blocks out a vast area of experience in Oriental man, from which undoubtedly many could learn with great profit. In the case of India, this is the whole pan-en-theistic current of thought, so beautifully exemplified in the *Gītā*, some *Upaniṣads*, the schools of Vaiṣṇavism, the Śaktivāda of the Hindu Tantras and in the remarkable South Indian system of Śaiva-Siddhānta. This proliferative movement was of cardinal importance in the making of India. By acting as a counter-balance to the other-worldliness of the monistic trends, it literally prevented the Indian culture from total self-extermination. For it is clear that the inevitable result for any culture which adopts a monistic philosophy as a common ideological basis must ultimately be suicide.

The present book is an introduction to the *Gītā*, the Magna Carta of Pan-en-theism, i.e. the teaching that all subsists in God without limiting Him. The *Gītā* has been styled a 'crisis book', since it was delivered on the morrow of one of the fiercest battles fought on Indian soil.* It is irrelevant whether or not this combat, as related in the *Mahābhārata*, is ascribed only partial historical reality, and whether or not the *Gītā* was actually revealed by a god-hero named Kṛṣṇa to a prince Arjuna. The *Gītā*'s unequivocal association with a crisis situation is all

* Shri Shankaracharya (Dr Kurtakoti), 'Towards a new world order—the Gitā', in *Studies in the Gītā*, ed. by M. D. Paradkar (Bombay, Popular Prakashan, 1970), p. 34.

that matters, and exactly because of this the gospel of Kṛṣṇa is destined to be of relevance today.

There are two main reasons which impelled me to write this book. Firstly, the existing literature on the *Gītā*, as vast as it is, does not appear congenial to the growing public demand for more serious presentations. There is a disconsolate dichotomy between outright academic studies which are of little or no appeal to the general reader, and the popular 'digests' which swamp the market. There are few books which seek to mediate between the scholar's preoccupation with predominantly theoretical-philological issues and the more concrete, life-orientated interests of the layman. The present book is an effort in this direction.

Secondly, over the past number of years my focal point of interest in Indian thought has gradually shifted from the purely metaphysical systems to the ethical teachings of Hinduism or, to put it differently, from *mokṣa-śāstra* to *dharma-śāstra*, from the culture of world-negation to that of world-affirmation. All Indian philosophical traditions agree that emancipation (*mokṣa*) is irrevocably the pinnacle of spiritual life. Nevertheless, it is *dharma* or 'moral order' which is recognised as the foundation and nutrient substratum of the path to deliverance. To bring this out is the principal objective of the *Gītā* and certainly one of the leading motives for writing this volume.

My study of the teachings of Kṛṣṇa has not been from the intellectual viewpoint only. As P. J. Saher once remarked:

> The attitude in some academic circles is that a philosopher is all the more to be praised, for being objective, the less he believes in the philosophy he is interpreting. The *Gītā*, however, is not a treatise which can be translated and commented upon by one who has not to some extent experienced the validity of its premises.*

I can but confirm the truth contained in these words. And I hope that some of the new insights I have gained through my own vivid and personally inspiring encounter with this ancient

*P. J. Saher, *Eastern Wisdom and Western Thought* (London, Allen & Unwin, 1969), p. 51.

tradition, and also my deep appreciation of it, will be conveyed in this book.

The material presented in this volume is arranged in such a manner as to guide the reader gradually to the central core of the gospel of Kṛṣṇa. In the first part he is introduced to the general cultural and historical context in which the *Gītā* is placed, as well as to the internal conditions of Vyāsa's work, with particular reference to its symbolism (a much neglected area). In the second part the wisdom-doctrine of Kṛṣṇa is set out as lucidly as these complex concepts permit.

It should require no special emphasis that the present treatment is far from being exhaustive and complete. In selecting a few specific paradigms, I merely hope to present and perhaps clarify some of the more important issues. In view of the massive bulk of literature on the *Gītā*, I can but agree with Professor Agehananda Bharati's contention that the *Gītā* is an 'overdone' topic of indological scholarship; however, I strongly feel that the quantity is remarkably disproportionate to the actual quality of the work that has been produced, and a fresh approach seems both warranted and desirable. If this book affords the student of the *Gītā* a more thorough glimpse of the practical and metaphysical intricacies of this unparalleled philosophical poem, then it has wholly fulfilled its purpose.

Finally, it remains for me to thank my friends Mrs. Caroline Tomlinson, M.A. and Mrs. Sunita Cutrara for their much appreciated help in preparing this book for the press: a time-consuming and little rewarding job. My sincere thanks are also due to Mrs. Doreen Barnett for her meticulous care in typing the manuscript. The person who has been of the greatest encouragement and inspiration is no longer among us. But if Kṛṣṇa is right in saying that

> never did I not exist, nor you . . . nor
> shall we [ever] be inexistent (II.12)

– then it is surely not too late to register my profound gratitude to Professor Jean Gebser.

Durham, 1974 G.A.F.

INTRODUCTION

I. THE HISTORICAL SIGNIFICANCE OF THE GĪTĀ IN INDIAN THOUGHT

The *Bhagavad-Gītā*, the 'Song of the Adorable One', is not only the most popular part of the canon of Hindu orthodoxy, but at the same time also a remarkable book on Yoga and one of the most touching documents of early philosophical and religious reflection. The *Gītā-Dhyāna*, a short eulogy often appended to the actual text of the *Gītā*, celebrates this archaic scripture as 'lotus of the Bhāratas' or *bhārata-paṅkaja*. The lotus flower is generally known as a symbol of purity and excellence.

In order to assess the real significance of the *Gītā* within the uncannily numerous philosophical and religious—the word 'gnostic' is perhaps preferable—movements which constitute the cultural heritage of India, it is desirable to outline its historical position with reference to both earlier and subsequent currents of thought. The intellectual and often the emotional appreciation of a thing depends to a marked degree on the availability of comparative material. This is even more so when, as in the present case, the subject in question is unfamiliar and highly intricate. Hence the following brief historical excursion.

The Vedic canonic literature, in which the *Gītā* is embedded like a jewel, is more comprehensive than any other religious canon on earth. It consists of the four old Vedic 'collections', the so-called *Saṃhitās*, the adjacent treatises elaborating the theory of sacrifice, i.e. the *Brāhmaṇas* and *Āraṇyakas*, as well as the *Upaniṣads*. These works embody traditions which were kept alive by oral transmission from earliest times. They are regarded as eternal revelation or *śruti* ('hearing'), as opposed to the corpus of texts compiled, under divine inspiration, by human authors and referred to as *smṛti* ('recollection').

The Vedic canon is pronounced to be of supra-human (*a-pauruṣeya*) origin. It is venerated as the work of the divine author of the world himself. *Veda* means 'gnostic knowledge' and as such is nothing else but the later *vidyā* or that supreme insight or enlightenment which leads to the shaking off of all fetters and ultimately to the realisation of the Supreme Essence of all things. The hymns of the *Veda* are esteemed to have been revealed to worthy seers or *ṛṣis* in a state of intensified awareness. The extreme beauty and rare insight and perception of many of the hymns speak in favour of this claim.

The four *Saṃhitās—Ṛgveda*, *Yajurveda*, *Sāmaveda* and *Atharvaveda*—are considered to be the earliest literary documents within the Indo-European sphere of thought. These archaic compilations form the foundation of all subsequent religious and philosophical traditions of India. By far the oldest 'collection' is the *Ṛgveda* which is, with its 1028 hymns, arranged in ten 'circles' or *maṇḍalas*. It is also the most voluminous hymnody. From the point of view of religious and philosophical ideas and their progressive development, this part of the ancient Vedic canon is the most significant and fecund. S. Radhakrishnan comments appreciatively:

> We find a freshness and simplicity and an inexplicable charm as of the breath of the spring or the flower of the morning about these first efforts of the human mind to comprehend and express the mystery of the world.[1*]

But more than with the mystifying workings of the universe, the early Indians were preoccupied with the nodal point in which this world rests—the primeval ground of all existence, the *brahman* of later periods. Hymns like the famous *puruṣa-sūkta*[2] and the equally renowned *nāsadīya-sūkta*[3] bear ready witness to this. Even though these hymns very probably do not represent the oldest strata of Vedic thought, the search for a

* Superior numbers in text refer to publications listed in the Notes to Text on pp. 167 to 171.

unifying principle, to which all manifoldness can be traced back, must have begun early on in the evolution of Indian philosophy.

Many of the hymns of the *Ṛgveda* were—and in some parts of India still are—used in the Vedic sacrifice to call the gods to participate in the sacred ritual. This was the office of the 'caller'-priest, the *hotṛ*.

The *Yajurveda*, the second collection of hymns, consists largely of hymns which have been absorbed from the *Ṛgveda*. These hymns, arranged systematically according to their function in the sacrificial ritual, were employed by the *adhvaryu* when preparing and offering the sacrifice.

The *Sāmaveda* contains mostly verses taken from the *Ṛgveda* which were sung by the *udgātṛ* during the *soma*-sacrifice. Together with the fire ritual, the cult of *soma* held the central position in the religious life of the Āryan immigrants who invaded Northern India about 3500 years ago. *Soma* is the name given to the divine draught which, when enjoyed, bestowed celestial powers and immortality on the sacrificer.

Last, the *Atharvaveda*, composed of about 6000 verses, served as a guide-book for the supervising priest, the *brāhmaṇa*. This collection is made up mainly of magical spells by which accidental mistakes occurring during the sacrifice could be neutralised so that no misfortune should befall those present. The philosophical and historical significance of the *Atharvaveda* is generally underestimated; it reflects a distinct and essential phase in the development of early Indian thought.

Despite the considerable progress in Vedic research since the days of Colebrooke and Max Müller, the spiritual content of the Vedic hymns has remained a sealed book to most contemporary interpreters. Predictably this situation will not be remedied until such time as it becomes more widely recognised that philology is an inadequate tool in deciphering 'spiritual hieroglyphs'.

The religious striving of the ancient Vedic people bore a vigorous world-affirmative stamp. To the Vedic Āryans the thought—typical for the classical Indian mind—of an emancipation from the world was entirely foreign. In the oldest portions of the *Ṛgveda* there are no indications of a world-negating seeking after God. Instead the great unknown numinous power behind the manifold phenomena was sought after by willingly accepting earthly life, through the referential and meticulously executed sacrificial rites, pure intentions, and the active and intrepid acceptance of the duties and responsibilities of daily life. This is touchingly expressed in the following hymn:

> Let us, ye gods, hear good [utterance],
> Let us with our eyes behold good [things],
> So that we who praisingly honour you
> May stride strong and vigorous through life.
>
> A hundred years are allotted to us on earth.
> Grant us this period which we have been foretold,
> So that we may watch sons become fathers.
> Do not tear us from our life's course.[4]

There was no trace of renunciation of worldly life, no belittlement of the life of a householder, or the pleasures, opportunities and attractions of this world. The picture which the most ancient hymns evoke in one's mind is one of a strong, healthy and innocent delight in the overflowing richness of nature. This does not mean that the old Vedic people indulged in unbridled debauchery and shameless gluttony. As so many hymns attest, they were anxious to align their lives with the grand Cosmic Order (*ṛta*), that universal harmony to which the orderly course of the seasons, the majestic movement of the stars and the inevitable alternation of day and night gave testimony. In a later hymn, a seer-poet prays:

> Lead us beyond all pain and grief along the path of *ṛta*.[5]

This *ṛta* is the key-concept within the philosophical framework of the Vedic people. As we shall see, in the guise of the concept of *dharma* ('norm') it preoccupied also the author of the *Gītā*. In fact, the dialogue between God Kṛṣṇa and the royal hero Arjuna is essentially nothing but an exposition of *dharma*. *Ṛta* is truth (*satya*), and it is truth which is said to uphold the three worlds—that of man, that of the forefathers and that of the gods. *Ṛta* is born out of the flame-power (*tapas*) by which the Primordial One exploded Itself into the multiplicity of living beings. In the *Aitareya-Brāhmaṇa* this idea is given expression in the form that Prajāpati, the Lord of Creatures, creates the universe by practising severe asceticism (*tapas*). Other old scriptures, also outside India, contain similar cosmogonic accounts.

Later another concept came to be intimately correlated with the idea of *ṛta* or 'order'; the sacrifice of *yajña*. Those hymns which may be regarded as the oldest excel the power and value of 'prayer' (*brahman*), and do not as yet show any sign of favouring sacrificial rites. The introduction of the sacrifice coincided with the growing organisation of the priesthood. The sacrifice was instituted in order to re-create the original wholeness, to repair the Creator symbolically, so that he might renewedly give his life for the sake of the world.

This idea is universal in the archaic world, and it springs from the peculiar ability or, perhaps, necessity of the archaic mind to correlate psychic with cosmic processes by way of analogy. Hence it is decidedly futile to speculate that the sacrifice might have been an invention of wily priests who by this innovation intended to secure for themselves a comfortable life in which the wine-skins were ever filled. However, the fact that the priestly élite endeavoured to establish a separatism and the supremacy of their own caste is a different matter altogether, which may justly be viewed from an economic angle.

The sectarianism of the ruling sacerdotal caste induced at an early stage a process of stagnation and torpidity which found its formal expression in the compilation of the *Brāhmaṇas*. These are prose works dealing with the most minute details of the Vedic ritual. In that period the sacrifice became more and more an end in itself. Finally, the *yajña* was given the rank of a transcendental power to which even the great multitude of gods of the Vedic pantheon was subordinate.

It was unavoidable that this class-conscious scholasticism and the unrestrained formalism of the priesthood should have given rise to antagonistic movements. These were, of course, eagerly fed by non-Āryan sources and gradually grew strong enough to seriously harass the brāhmaṇical orthodoxy. So as not to be uprooted, the priestly élite reacted by yielding to this enormous pressure and by assimilating decisive elements from the autochtoneous cultures.

The first anti-brāhmaṇical tendencies are already apparent in the *Āraṇyakas*. These are esoteric texts, similar to the *Brāhmaṇas*, which—according to later tradition—served the hermit as books of ritual and mystery. The process of assimilation of the non-Āryan cultures into the fold of Brāhmaṇism reached its culmination, around 900 B.C., with the coming of the *Upaniṣads*.

The *Upaniṣads* are considered the acme of the Vedic revelation. They are gnostic treatises which, on the one hand, teach the fundamental dictum of the essential unity of all beings, moving or unmoving, and, on the other hand, have the practical purpose of inspiring the student to tread the path towards the experiental realisation of this *unio mystica*.

The word *upaniṣad* can be derived from the two prefixes *upa* and *ni* and the verbal root √*sad* (which is suggestive of the word *sat* 'to be, Being' used for the Primordial Reality and derived from the root √*as* 'to be'); it has the meaning of 'to sit close to', which probably contains a reference to the form in which the gnostic doctrine was orally transmitted from teacher to disciple. Hence, in a figurative sense the term *upaniṣad* means as much as 'secret teaching' or *rahasya*. If one takes account of the cognate word *sat* (= *brahman*), an *Upaniṣad* would accordingly be a secret doctrine by which a man is approximated to Being.

This approximation to Being, which should ultimately grow

into a deep connection, even union, is the central motive of Indian thought.

Here are a few characteristic passages from the *Upaniṣads*:

Now, that which is the Self (*ātman*) is the dam (*setu*), the separation for keeping-apart these worlds. This dam is not crossed by day or night, not by old age, not by death, not by sorrow, not by well-doing, not by wrong-doing. From that all evils turn back, for that *brahman*-world is devoid of evil.

Therefore when crossing that dam, a blind [person] is no [longer] blind, a wounded is no [longer] wounded, an afflicted is no [longer] afflicted. Hence, verily, when crossing that dam, the night turns into day. For that *brahman*-world is ever luminous.[6]

Seizing as a bow the great weapon of the *Upaniṣad*, one should adjust an arrow [on it] sharpened by meditation (*upāsāna*). Stretching it with a mind absorbed (*gata*) in the state-of-being of That [Ultimate Reality], penetrate that Imperishable as the mark, o *soma*-inspired one.

The *praṇava* [i.e. the monosyllable *oṃ*] is the bow. Oneself (*ātman*) is the arrow. *Brahman* is sad to be that mark. It is to be penetrated by [him who is] attentive. He should become united with it (*tan-maya*), like an arrow [which hits the target].[7]

Simultaneously (*ekadhā*) only is This Indemonstrable, Immutable [Being] to be seen. [That which is] pure, higher than the ether, unborn—[that is] the Great Immutable Self (*ātman*).

Knowing Him, a wise *brāhmaṇa* should employ gnosis-knowledge (*prajñā*): He should not ponder about many words, for that is injury to speech.[8]

To bring man closer to the Supreme Being is the primary intent also of the *Gītā*. In this respect its upaniṣadic character is irrefutable, and the colophon at the end of each of its eighteen songs needs no correction. Yet officially the *Gītā* is counted as a work of the *smṛti* genre, as is the *Mahābhārata* epic of which it is part. Wherein the *Gītā* differs from the general tone of the *Upaniṣads* is in its decidedly theistic outlook. The *Upaniṣads*, on the whole, propagate a philosophy which is pure Monism; there is only the One Reality which, to the unenlightened mind, appears as many. This is admittedly also the underlying concept of the philosophy of the *Gītā*. However, the *Gītā* strives to make this Absolute One tangible to the human mind in the form of the charioteer Kṛṣṇa, in truth the incarnation of the Divine, the embodiment of the omnipresent Viṣṇu.

The *Upaniṣads* portray clearly to what extent the Indian sages were concerned with apprehending this Supreme Reality in ever more precise circumlocutions. To them, this was far more than a mere exercise in substantiating and demonstrating logically the validity of their profound insights and experiences. Although the *Upaniṣads* are full of logical and mythological speculations about this One Reality and its relationship to the phenomenal world, these utterances are more of the nature of spontaneous verbalisations of what stirred the heart and mind of the individual seer, rather than clever philosophising. Philosophical insight and knowledge had to prove good and useful in practice. The intuition that all appearances have one common substratum, the *brahman*, had to be re-transformed into unmediated experience. For, only he who attained total intimacy with the One, who has become the One, was emancipated from the fetters of the Many. As the *Upaniṣad* says:

> Verily, he who know that supreme *brahman*, becomes [that] very *brahman*.[9]

The path which the upaniṣadic sages adopted was one of progressive negation, practical as well as philosophical. By uncovering gradually the impermanence of the Many, they opened the view to the One. Hand in hand with this insight went the practice of renunciation of all that had been revealed as Many, as impermanent and sorrowful. This tendency of complete negation appears strange and distorted to the Western reader. Often he cannot avoid the impression that the *Upaniṣads* are too removed from the concerns of this world—as indeed they are—to be inspiring at all. Rightly, Juan Mascaró

called them 'himalayas of the soul', for they are indeed like those far-off snow-covered peaks towering high above ordinary life.

The 'climate' of the *Gītā* is completely different. It contrasts the cool, lofty transcendentalism of the *Upaniṣads* with a tangible, vivifying Theism. It stands as a genuine mediator between this transient world and that Supreme Reality whose distant glow it endeavours to reflect.

Historically, the *Gītā* is of paramount importance for the whole development of the so-called post-Vedic thought. Its popularity among the creative élite of the Indian people can be seen in the fact that again and again it was used as the archetype for similar poetic-philosophical creations. It is, of course, understandable that none of the numerous *Gītā* imitations has ever equalled the original.

The *Gītā* is composed of not more than 700 stanzas. And all orthodox schools of Indian philosophy are based on this, seemingly insignificant, conglomeration of didactic verses. Scarcely any of the leading thinkers of Hinduism scrupled to ignore the *Gītā*. Whoever intended to establish a new system or school had to understand how to sanction it through the Vedic canon and the *Gītā*. Disregard for the ancient sacred tradition simply meant heresy; it was punished by expulsion from the Hindu social order. On the other hand, incomparable tolerance was exercised towards all those who, whilst stepping boldly into new areas of thought, showed fidelity to the Vedic tradition.

Thus it was possible for a revolutionary like Īśvara Kṛṣṇa (second century A.D.?) to establish quite safely his atheistic Sāṃkhya system, for Madhva to propound his Dualism and for Śaṅkara to preach his extreme Non-dualism. Although these schools entertained contradictory points of view which were in no way reconcilable with the original Vedic revelation, they were nevertheless delegated a respectable place within the 'hospitable mansion' (A. C. Bouquet) of Vedic-Hinduistic culture, because their founders acknowledged the revelatory contents of the Vedas.

In this strict acceptance of the Vedic tradition the preserving character of the Indian mentality comes distinctly to the fore. This intriguing quality of the Indian mind finds its expression in varied ways. For example, it manifests unmistakably in the stress laid on the worship of the forefathers (*pitṛ*); it is also exposed in the famous theory of the world-ages (*yuga*). Possibly nowhere on this globe has the past ruled the imagination and stirred the heart of man as much as it did in India. No other people have shown a similar aptitude for negating the present and reversing history by trying with great zeal and admirable consistency to locate a path back to the Origin, the source of all time. The return to the Supramundane Unity, the reinstatement of man to the wholeness of paradise, of which all archaic peoples dreamt, was nowhere taken more seriously and striven for more persistently than in India. Yoga, as a 'science' of achieving this transformation of finite man into the infinite One, has to be recognised as something intrinsically Indian or, as Mircea Eliade put it, as 'a specific dimension of the Indian mind'.

The popularity of any book, philosophical or religious, can in the case of India be measured by the extent of the commentary literature which grew around it in the course of time. And the number of commentaries to the *Gītā* is legend. The oldest extant commentary is the *Bhāṣya* of Śaṅkara Ācārya, the eminent exponent of Advaita-Vedānta.

As expected, the great teacher interprets the *Gītā* in the light of his own philosophy. His commentary is not only biased, but altogether a disappointing piece of work which compares badly with his elaborate and thoughtful commentary on the *Brahma-Sūtra* of Bādarāyaṇa. It is fairly certain that the *Gītā* was interpreted previously to Śaṅkara, as the *ācārya* himself refers to former commentaries at the outset of his own work.

Śaṅkara is supposed to have lived from A.D. 788 to 820. Considering the immense wealth of literary-scholastic writings he bequeathed to India, it seems rather improbable that he should have died at the age of thirty-two. At any rate, Śaṅkara

was a prolific writer and an ardent missionary of great popularity. He may be regarded as one of the most influential, though not necessarily the most original, of Indian thinkers. His Non-dualism withstood the multiple attacks from Buddhist and Jainist quarters and also survived the massive encounter with the pan-en-theistic current of thought within the Hindu orthodoxy. In fact, it has become the dominant trend in the philosophy of modern Hinduism. The other orthodox systems (*darśana*), like the Sāṃkhya and the Classical Yoga of Patañjali, were either dislodged from their formerly powerful position by this mighty intellectual construction, or simply reduced to playing an insignificant role in contemporary Indian philosophical speculation.

Śaṅkara was not so much a reformer as a propagator who set his gigantic intellect to work towards the establishment of the truth of Unqualified Monism. The philosophical doctrine itself was not of his making, and he himself admits that his teacher's teacher Gauḍapāda (seventh century A.D.?) had 'recovered' it from the Vedas. Śaṅkara saw it as his function to prove beyond all doubt that this doctrine was indeed the sole contention of the *Upaniṣads* and the *Brahma-Sūtra*, a compilation of aphorisms of extreme brevity based on the *Upaniṣads* and probably written in the second century A.D. Śaṅkara may have been a would-be philosopher, but he was certainly a brilliant exegetist and a devoted and painstaking scholar, as well as a laudable disputant.

Like Kant, with whom he is not infrequently compared, Śaṅkara wished once and for all to settle the matter of metaphysics and to place all previous philosophising into proper perspective. By assuming a Transcendental Idealism, Śaṅkara paralysed the poignant arguments of his opponents, which, as he relentlessly pointed out, were merely from the 'lower', i.e. phenomenological viewpoint, and therefore did not embody absolute truth. It is difficult to assess to what extent Śaṅkara contributed to the gradual increase of aridity in the intellectual and social life of India. Certainly his philosophy, being in a way beyond dispute, contained no antidote against the advance of the attitude of world-negation. On the contrary, Śaṅkara's metaphysics presented as it were the *raison d'être* for this increasing indifference towards mundane values and things.

This weariness with worldly life made itself felt for the first time in the earliest *Upaniṣads*, almost one millennium before the great *ācārya*'s time. One may also surmise that this very attitude had long before been the cause responsible for the downfall of the empire that flourished in the Indus valley. This melancholic outlook, imbued with a nostalgic longing for the Reality which lies eternally beyond the dreamlike phenomena of this world, is, one might presume, part of the inheritance from the indigenous non-Āryan peoples. For the Āryan immigrants were a strong and vital people; how else could they have achieved their remarkable conquest?

Already the Buddha (500 B.C.) was accused of tearing away men from their wives, sons from their mothers, and turning them into monks. By the time of Śaṅkara, more than a millennium later, the life of the renunciant or *saṃnyāsin* had become the crowning ideal, so much so, that the monasteries became overcrowded and the streets of the villages and towns were lined with mendicant monks and beggars in the guise of monks. To this very day this picture has not changed.

Śaṅkara is the embodiment of the continuous readiness of the Indian mind to renounce the Many in favour of the One. As such he symbolises the exact antithesis to Kṛṣṇa, the propounder of the sublime philosophy of the *Gītā*, whose doctrine is one of life- and world-affirmation. These two disparate attitudes are the propelling forces underlying the proliferous unfoldment of Indian thought and life. When viewed from this bi-polarity, the intricate pattern of Indian philosophical and religious growth begins to be more intelligible and deeply instructive.

Since Śaṅkara, in his attempt to reconcile his philosophy with the statements of the Sacred Scriptures, could not afford to overlook the *Gītā* as the most popular part of the *prasthāna-traya* or triple canon of Hinduism, he had to twist its philosophy to suit his own purposes. In this approach he was by no means

alone in his native land. Indeed are there not also exact parallels in European theology and philosophy? We only need to remember the multitude of Christian churches which base their establishment on the Bible or the New Testament.

For Śaṅkara, the One appears to be manifold only on account of nescience (*avidyā*), which in itself is undefinable. The world is merely a mutation of this nescience, a distortion (*vivarta*) of the Supreme Reality. Man and the cosmos are shadow-phenomena, with no absolute significance, and hence have to be eschewed and surpassed by way of knowing and becoming the One. They are like an imaginary snake which is in reality a rope. In his *Viveka-Cūḍāmaṇi*, Śaṅkara formulates it succinctly thus:

> A pot, though a modification of clay, is not different [from it]; because [the pot] is everywhere essentially clay...[Similarly], the whole [world], as a modification of the real *brahman*, is but that real [*brahman*]...[10]

In a system which stresses the *unreality* (not non-existence!) of the world, any human action must ultimately be considered futile. Śaṅkara takes great pains to emphasise this point wherever an opportunity presents itself. Action (*karman*) cannot destroy ignorance. Only the fire of gnosis (*jñāna*) can burn nescience to ashes and emancipate man from his self-imposed bondage. Śaṅkara could not possibly have approved of Arjuna's course of action, namely to participate in a most gruesome battle. Consequently, he regarded the hero of the *Gītā* as unfit for the sublime truth of Non-dualism (*a-dvaita*)—thus distorting the central message of the *Gītā* itself. But Śaṅkara's absolute Idealism and his radical reinterpretation, not to say misinterpretation, were not left unchallenged.

In the eleventh century A.D., Rāmānuja founded the Viśiṣṭa-Advaita or 'Non-dualism of the Differentiated', which, in turn, gave birth to a host of other schools advocating a moderate Non-dualism in contradistinction to the unconditional Monism of Śaṅkara. In addition to commentaries on some of the *Upaniṣads*, and on the *Brahma-Sūtra*, Rāmānuja also wrote a brief commentary on the *Gītā*. After an unsuccessful marriage, Rāmānuja devoted his life entirely to teaching. His activities led to considerable and encouraging social reforms. His philosophy proved a strong bulwark against the total usurpation of Indian culture by the doctrines of non-dualistic Vedānta. Rāmānuja elaborated and consolidated the ancient teachings of Vaiṣṇavism, as embedded in the *Pāñcarātra-Saṃhitās*, the *Bhāgavata-* and the *Viṣṇu-Purāṇa* and parts of the *Mahābhārata*, and enriched and incited the already popular devotional (*bhakti*) movement. Rāmānuja himself was a great *bhakta*, completely devoted to the ideal of 'caritas' and piety.

For him, the One Reality was not a Void without qualities, as Śaṅkara and the Mahāyāna Buddhists visualised it, but he taught the *brahman* to comprise innumerable qualities, above all the quality of love (*bhakti*). Rāmānuja, like Śaṅkara a mouthpiece of old traditions, firmly rejected the idea of the illusoriness of the world. To him, creation is real beyond all doubt. But creation is not something external to the Creator; the Supreme Reality is both creator and created, knower and known. The many individual beings and the world in which they live are the members of the body of God.

Rāmānuja's thought is true to the metaphysical outlook of the *Gītā*. This is not astonishing, since the *Gītā* itself belongs to the Vaiṣṇava tradition. In his commentary, Rāmānuja has tried to retrieve the *Gītā*'s spirit from the icy logical world of Śaṅkara and return it to the reality of the human world. Still, his stress on *bhakti* or love for God—which he held to be the essential method taught in the *Gītā*—has partially blinded him to the ethical teachings of the *Gītā*. Rāmānuja has, however, given a fresh impetus to Theism, and the centuries following him witnessed a great revival of theistic thought and the intimately related *bhakti* cult, particularly in Southern India.

Among the more illustrious Vaiṣṇava teachers and preachers were Nimbārka (eleventh century A.D.), Madhva (1197–1273), Nām-deva (1269–95), Jñāneśvar (1275–96) and Rāmānanda

(1360–1450), who started the Vaiṣṇava movement in the North. Rāmānanda's disciple was the famous Kābir (1440–1518), who, in turn, inspired Guru Nānak (1469–1538), the founder of the Sikh school. One of the most remarkable personages was Caitanya (1485–1533), the founder of the school of the Bheda-Abheda-Vāda. Arguing that the simultaneous identity and difference between God, souls and material world transcend human understanding, he called on his disciples and followers to seek the direct connection with God by way of self-sacrificing devotion or love (*prema*). His gospel fell into the time of the worst Moslem invasions and was received with gratitude and enthusiasm by innumerable people. Because of his outstanding saintliness he came to be regarded even in his lifetime as one of the incarnations (*avatāra*) of God Viṣṇu.

The *Gītā* never had an effective philosophical school of its own. Rather it is the direct expression of the philosophy or life-style of a section of India's culture. It is a living witness to the ever-present, though often undermined, trend in Indian thought to do justice to the organic wholeness and complexity of life.

The *Gītā* gives lie to all those sweeping generalisations of uninformed Western critics who profess Indian history to be one long-drawn-out and pertinacious attempt to opt out of the realities of this world. The *Gītā* is the revival of a life-style the beginnings of which date back to the earliest Vedic times and which was never really lost sight of in the long development of Indian culture, although the onslaught of Transcendentalism with its categoric demand for unflinching asceticism and total renunciation has often obscured this old teaching. Already Bhīṣma, a nobleman and leading figure in the great war between the Kurus and the Pāñcalas, complained bitterly that fewer and fewer people respected the old tradition of *dharma*,[11] and that they seemed all too keen to discard social ties and responsibilities and flee into the forest.[12]

From that early period on, the idea of world-renunciation obsessed Indian man with ever increasing vigour. The climax of this whole Parmenidian trend was reached in Śaṅkara, who tried to sanction it philosophically by means of his doctrine of the unreality (*māyā*) of the world of multiplicity. However, a philosophical denial of the reality of the world does not change its practical actuality impinging on man's everyday life. This is best illustrated in an anecdote told about Śaṅkara himself:

A king, to whom Śaṅkara had expounded his doctrine of the unreality of the phenomenal universe, was curious to ascertain to what degree this teaching was rooted in Śaṅkara's own mind. Hence, when Śaṅkara next asked for an audience with the king, the monarch ordered a mad elephant to be released. As the philosopher saw the animal charging at him, he began to run as fast as his legs would bear him, and he would not stop till he had found a safe place. Panting for breath and perspiring, but mentally serene, Śaṅkara appeared before the king, who reproached him for having run away from what he should have recognised as a mere illusion. Śaṅkara's reply is characteristic: 'In truth, neither the elephant is real, nor you, nor I. It was merely an illusion of yours that you saw me escape from the elephant.'

It was inevitable that there should arise a keen demand for a philosophy which would take into full account the concrete situations of life. Radical Non-dualism leaves no space for a personal relationship with the Divine. Even the most noble of emotions, unselfconscious love, becomes illusory. Everything human is denied. For, the One is without qualities (*nir-guṇa*). People longed for a tangible philosophy of life, and this led to the great reanimation of pan-en-theistic doctrines and the creation of the *bhakti* movement which persisted till the seventeenth century. The *Gītā* was given the place of honour amidst this vasṭ and diversified movement. And, in a way, it represented the grand ideal—often aspired to, but never really attained. S. Radhakrishnan echoes the opinion of many when he says:

> The message of the Gītā is universal in its scope.[13]

Śrī Aurobindo, the father of Integral Yoga, elucidates:

In the Gītā there is very little that is merely local or temporal and its spirit is so large, profound and universal that even this little can easily be universalised without the sense of the teaching suffering any diminution or violation; rather by giving an ampler scope to it than belonged to the country and epoch, the teaching gains in depth, truth and power.[14]

II. THE DATE OF THE GĪTĀ

Unlike the Chinese, who have always displayed a lively interest in recording history, the Indian people lack, to the scholar's constant dismay and frustration, all sense of history. Surely, the *Purāṇas*—ancient works on cosmogony, mythology and philosophy—cannot be counted as proper histories, although the historical value of the genealogies of royal houses which they contain has often been underrated. The student of Indian philosophy and religion is confronted with a vast literature comprising infinite traditions whose chronology is in almost all cases absolutely conjectural. Furthermore, as a rule nothing is handed down about the personal life of the founder of schools or systems, or the composers of literary or scientific works.

The *Gītā* is no exception. Scholars have gone to considerable trouble and have shown much ingenuity in ascertaining the date of the *Gītā*; yet the divergent conclusions at which they arrive demonstrate beyond all doubt how impossible it is to fix a definite point in time for any particular event in this massive stream of knowledge, flowing from the time of the *Vedas*, and earlier, uninterruptedly down to the present age.

One of the main reasons for the indologist's failure in his chronological computations is that he is apparently oblivious to the fact that Indian thought, until comparatively recently, was not committed to pen, and that therefore he pre-eminently deals with *oral* traditions to which *textual* criticism does not strictly apply. The truth of this observation becomes singularly apparent in the example of the *Gītā* which is only a minute fragment of a much larger oral tradition, *viz* that of the *Mahābhārata*. The reference in the first book of the *Mahābhārata* to the elephant-headed god Gaṇeśa, who is said to have written down the epic to the dictation of Vyāsa, is assuredly a later interpolation; this addition must have been made at a time when the cult of Gaṇeśa had already become fully established, possibly in the ninth century A.D. Besides, the direct disciples of Vyāsa, the author of the great epic, supposedly learned the *Mahābhārata* by heart. Although writing appears to have been known already in the seventh century B.C., it is highly unlikely that it was employed in other than mundane contexts. To isolate the *Gītā* and treat it as a distinct textual entity, independent of the main body of the epic, is a fallacious undertaking.

The indologist is constantly confronted with the paradoxical situation that works whose language and style point to their later date, reflect in fact genuine ancient traditions. The *Gītā* characterises itself as 'ancient teaching' (IV.3), and few scholars today would deny that its 'original form'—whatever that may be—belongs to the pre-Christian era. There have been many attempts to pinpoint the date more accurately, and the various speculations differ widely both in the depth of their analysis and in their end-product. In a recent study on the *Gītā*, this topic has been ably re-examined, and the author, K. N. Upadhyaya, summarised his findings thus:

> ...we can reasonably conclude that the Bhagavadgītā was composed sometime between the 5th and 4th century B.C. when the growing impact of Buddhism, besides that of the Upaniṣads, had made it essential for the orthodox tradition to resuscitate and vindicate its position by making necessary adjustments and modifications in its thoughts. By combining the various strands of thought, both old and new, the Gītā presents a compromising philosophy, and thereby tries to counteract the growing influence of atheism and renunciation advocated by Buddhism, Jainism and other contemporary currents of thought.[15]

The question of the date of the *Gītā* involves several other highly problematic issues, such as whether the *Gītā* constituted an integral part of the *Mahābhārata* from the very beginning, and whether or not it has undergone any alterations and additions in the course of time. This is not the place to enter into a detailed discussion of these vexed questions. In view of the subsequent remarks about the internal structure of the *Gītā*, however, it seems apposite to state briefly the position held by the present author. The *Gītā* has often been dissected and split into so many sub-texts. The renowned German historian of religion, Rudolf Otto, even succeeded in reducing it to two-thirds of its size before he was convinced that he had found the 'original' *Gītā*. In a more recent work the *Gītā* is earmarked as the patchwork of three authors who wrote in different centuries.[16]

Diverse claims have also been made about its origin. Once it was held to be a treatise on Sāṃkhyayoga revised by followers of the Kṛṣṇa-Vasudeva cult, then again it was considered a pantheistic poem remodelled in the light of Vaiṣṇavism, then again an *Upaniṣad* adapted to the Kṛṣṇa worship, and so on. All these hypotheses, and they are no more than that, disregard two all-important points:

1. There are numerous references to the *Gītā* scattered throughout the *Mahābhārata.*
2. There is a remarkable agreement between the *Gītā* and the epic in the use of words, their language and thought. (This point has been convincingly demonstrated by G. Tilak.)

In the face of these pressing facts, any assumption other than that the *Gītā* does indeed constitute an integral part of the *Mahābhārata* would be illogical and unconvincing. Taking all the various points into consideration, it seems most probable that the *Gītā* has never been a distinct textual entity, but that it belongs intrinsically to the Vaiṣṇava tradition of the epic. The second question as to whether the *Gītā* has passed through successive stages of elaboration and enlargement, again, has been satisfactorily answered by K. N. Upadhyaya:

It must not be forgotten that unlike other predominantly historical and semi-historical portions of the Mahābhārata, the Gītā was meant to serve a definite didactic purpose. With regard to the former, insertion of so many stories and narratives (Upākhyānas) linked one way or the other with the main theme could be easily possible. But a predominantly didactic work like the Gītā could hardly make room for such insertions. So if insertions and additions are supposed to have been made in the Gītā, they, in all probability, would have been of an elaborative and explicatory nature.[17]

Scholars have found it difficult to accept the view that the *Gītā* has been preserved more or less in its original form. Their principal objection concerns the apparent inconsistencies in the doctrines of the *Gītā*. But on closer examination these alleged incompatibilities of ideas prove to be largely due to the scholar's interpretation of the language of the *Gītā* in the light of later thought, when certain terms—such as *yoga*, *sāṃkhya* and *vedānta*—had already assumed a well-defined technical meaning.

The *Gītā* is not a systematic treatise on philosophy, else it could hardly have been written in verse.[18] It is, as Juan Mascaró rightly points out, a 'spiritual poem'; justly he adds: 'and as such it must be judged; and it must be seen as a whole'.[19] As Professor S. Dasgupta confirms:

> The *Gītā*...is not to be looked upon as a properly schemed system of philosophy, but as a manual of right conduct and right perspective of things in the light of a mystical approach to God in self-resignation, devotion, friendship and humility.[20]

Hence different criteria have to be used to come to an understanding of the concepts and the imagery of the *Gītā*. It has to be approached with the same wide, tolerant attitude which it displays itself and which makes it so attractive for the modern reader.

III. VYĀSA—POET AND PHILOSOPHER

While in most countries a history of philosophy is inseparable from a history of philosophers, in India we have indeed ample materials for watching the origin and growth of philosophical ideas, but hardly any for studying the lives or characters of those who founded or supported the philosophical system of that country.[21]

The reason for this evidently lies in the peculiar mental horizon of the Indian people in which there is little room for the closely related concepts of individuality and of history. To the classical Indian mind it is absolutely irrelevant at which moment in history and under what conditions an event takes place. His sole interest is directed towards the intrinsic value, the essential quality, of that event. Hence there is a disheartening lack of records about those creative minds who have been vital in the shaping of the Indian culture. Usually the scanty biographical details that are available consist of no more than a handful of legends which are again representative only of the essential nature of the individual in question, not of his real, historic form.

This also applies to Vyāsa, whom tradition credits with the authorship of the *Gītā* and the whole of the *Mahābhārata*. In addition to this epic creation, which incidentally is also the most comprehensive in existence, he is also connected with the authorship of the *Purāṇas*—a huge mass of writings for all those who were excluded from the study of the *Vedas*—the *Brahma-Sūtra* (generally ascribed to Bādarāyaṇa) and, strangely enough, a commentary on the *Yoga-Sūtra* of Patañjali. Considering the extent of the varied character as also the chronological spacing of this voluminous literature, it is hardly credible that any one person should have been able to compile all these works within his life-span. These and similar deliberations have induced a number of scholars to doubt the historicity of Vyāsa altogether and to view him as an entirely legendary figure. However, this conclusion is only an elegant way of avoiding a more painstaking analysis of this particular set of problems. The facts at hand point to a more plausible hypothesis, namely that Vyāsa was an extraordinarily gifted personage who regarded it as his life's task to collect and edit, at the fringe of the brāhmaṇical orthodoxy, the mythological, religious, philosophical and folkloristic traditions belonging or adjacent to the early Vaiṣṇava movement on the basis of the great epic story of the tribal war that took place at the beginning of the first millennium B.C.

Vyāsa, like Homer, surely had no scholarly intentions in his compilatory activities. Rather he was deeply concerned with keeping popular traditions alive, so that they would be an unceasing inspiration in the daily life of his contemporaries and that of subsequent generations. Vyāsa wrote out of that timeless plenitude to which all the great philosophical and religious geniuses of India seem to have had free access. His work is the expression of deepest psycho-spiritual truths. This is also the only sound explanation for the enormous popularity which the *Mahābhārata* together with the *Gītā* has enjoyed throughout the ages, for the historical actualities of the epic—which in any case are probably minimal—could never have retained the enthusiasm of any people, least of all the totally unhistorical Indians, for so long.

The *Mahābhārata* contains several allusions to Vyāsa's life, unless they are later interpolations for which there is no evidence at all. These supply us with some interesting information about this illustrious bard and sage. As with the remainder of the *Mahāḅhārata*, it is not clear how much of Vyāsa's 'autobiographical notes' is true to history and how much legendary or symbolical. Yet whoever attempts to abstract from these scattered statements 'historical truth' has to bear in mind that Vyāsa, no doubt already famous in his lifetime, would have had little reason to 'invent' an autobiography in full, particularly in view of the fact that it was not at all in his favour. The following is an epitome of the account of Vyāsa's life as found in the great epic itself.[22]

Vyāsa was born the son of the sage Parāśara ('destroyer') and the lovely fisher maiden Satyavatī ('truthful one'). One day Satyavatī, who was in charge of her father's ferry, had to take the seer Parāśara across the river. When the sage saw the extreme loveliness of the girl, his heart was set ablaze with passion for her, and he could not resist making advances. Satyavatī rebuffed his attempts courteously but firmly. Yet when the persistent ascetic promised her that she need not fear losing her maidenhood, she finally consented to reciprocate his passion. Parāśara also gave his word to transform the unpleasant fish odour from which she suffered since her birth into a bewitching fragrance which would never leave her again. In order that they might express their love unseen by the many ascetics and mendicants camping on both sides of the river, the sage caused a thick fog to envelop the river valley. That same day Satyavatī gave birth to a son without suffering the loss of her virginity.

Because the child was born on the island Jumnā in the river Yamunā, he was called Dvaipāyana, 'island-born', and Kṛṣṇa, 'black one', on account of his dark complexion. The young boy immediately turned to the practice of severe asceticism (*tapas*), and in due course attained great powers. Having gained the insight that the morality of mankind would diminish with each future world-age (*yuga*), he resolved to collect and explain the Vedic revelation. This brought him the name Vyāsa, 'collector'. Vyāsa led the meagre life of an ascetic. However, when his stepbrother passed away unexpectedly, his mother Satyavatī, who by then had married the Kuru king Śāntanu, asked him to take the responsibility for the continuation of the lineage. Vyāsa obeyed, and so it happened that the two childless wives of his deceased stepbrother both gave birth to a boy each, Dhṛtarāṣṭra and Pāṇḍu. They, as is well known, were the fathers of the heroes who waged war against each other on the ill-famed *kuru-kṣetra*.

Vyāsa is evidently the creator of the figures whose course of life he himself traces in the epic story. His characters are figments of his imagination or, which seems more likely, that their specific personalities are shaped by him, no matter what their historical basis might have been. In favour of this hypothesis is, among other criteria, also the fact that it is Vyāsa himself, who, towards the end of the sixteenth chapter of the epic, announces that the time has come for the Pāṇḍavas to prepare for death. Vyāsa here acts suspiciously like a playwright who stage manages his own play.

In the epic Vyāsa is described as exceedingly ugly. In fact, one of the widows of his departed stepbrother was so repulsed by the sight of him that she unwittingly closed her eyes when he approached her. Vyāsa, in great anger, cursed the poor woman. The fruit of their union was the blind-born king Dhṛtarāṣṭra. However, these disadvantageous external attributes of Vyāsa did not prevent the Indian people from celebrating him as the ideal of wisdom and holiness and even from venerating him as an embodiment of the supreme God Viṣṇu himself.

According to a widespread belief, Vyāsa never died. He is said to live on in his hermitage Badarī in the Himalayas where he can be found by all who have advanced in their meditative practices.

The epic states that Vyāsa composed the *Mahābhārata* within a period of only three years and dictated it to the sagacious god Gaṇeśa, who was the only one able to follow the swiftness of his thoughts. The *Mahābhārata* was first recited, by Vyāsa's pupil Vaiśampāyana, at the great snake-sacrifice of the king Janamejaya Pārikṣita. Vyāsa taught the epic to his son Śuka and five of his disciples who were all asked to write down their version of it and only Vaiśampāyana's compilation turned out to be agreeable to Vyāsa.

Vyāsa is mentioned three times in the *Bhagavad-Gītā*, the spiritual nucleus of the epic; once as a seer (*ṛṣi*, X.13), then as a sage (*muni*, X.37), and in the last chapter actually as the author of the *Gītā*. The last-mentioned instance deserves our full attention.

By the grace of Vyāsa, I heard this supreme, secret Yoga from the Lord of Yoga, Kṛṣṇa, Himself speaking before my very eyes.[23]

This stanza is spoken by Saṃjaya, who relates the *Gitā* to the blind king Dhṛtarāṣṭra. The meaning of this verse seems to be that through the grace (*prasāda*) or yogic power of Vyāsa, Saṃjaya was able to witness the momentous discourse between Kṛṣṇa and Arjuna. Śaṅkara, in his commentary on the *Gītā*, elucidates that Vyāsa had bestowed on Saṃjaya the *divya-cakṣus* or 'divine eye'. Nataraja Guru, a recent interpreter and translator of the *Gītā*, offers a more acceptable explanation. Going on the assumption that the *Gītā* is an integral part of the epic, he says:

...Vyāsa puts his own real signature to the treatise, just as an artist might initial the corner of a painting. Indirectly, he wants to make it clear that all that was reported by Sanjaya to the blind king Dhritarāshtra as actually having transpired objectively, had its original prototype in the words of Vyāsa himself.[24]

This interpretation is entirely congruous with the evidence found in the *Mahābhārata*: Vyāsa manipulates, and participates in, the drama which he himself unfolds in such a manner that it is subtly but firmly impressed on the reader's mind that he, Vyāsa, holds the key to the future of his heroes.

The picture that gradually emerges is that of a sage who—ahead of his time—has placed his great knowledge and learning at the disposal of his people. In the words of S. Radhakrishnan:

[Vyāsa] is a man of deep culture, catholic rather than critical. He does not lead a missionary movement; he addresses no sect, establishes no school, but opens the way to all the winds that blow. He sympathises with all forms of worship, and is therefore well fitted for the task of interpreting the spirit of Hinduism which is unwilling to break up culture into compartments and treat other forms of thought and practices in a spirit of negation...The tone of the

Gītā is dogmatic, and its author does not suspect that it is possible for him to err. He gives the truth as he sees it, and he seems to see it in its entirety and many-sidedness, and to believe in its saving power.[25]

Śrī Aurobindo observes:

The language of the Gita, the structure of thought, the combination and balancing of ideas belong neither to the temper of a sectarian teacher nor to the spirit of a rigorous analytical dialectics cutting off one angle of the truth to exclude all the others; but rather there is a wide, undulating, encircling movement of ideas which is the manifestation of a vast synthetic mind and a rich synthetic experience.[26]

IV. THE MAHĀBHĀRATA

The *Gītā* comprises of sections 13–40 of the so-called *bhīṣma-parvan*, the sixth book, of the *Mahābhārata*. This seems reason enough to direct our attention briefly to this grand epic.

India, like Greece, has produced two gigantic epics, the *Rāmāyaṇa* and the *Mahābhārata*. The *Rāmāyaṇa*, or the 'Life of Rāma', treats in 24,000 stanzas the legend of the divine hero Rāma, his combat with daemonic forces and the recovery of his wife Sītā, who had been abducted by Rāvaṇa, the king of the netherworld Laṅkā (Ceylon?). The incredible wealth of episodes and stories, woven into this mammoth work like a colourful patterned carpet, edify and delight the people of India even today. Whereas the *Mahābhārata* insists on belonging to *smṛti* or sacred tradition, the *Rāmāyaṇa* contends to be no more than poetry (*kāvya*). And as such it has served later generations of poets as a celebrated prototype for their own creations. Śrī Aurobindo, who has perhaps known the life-pulse of Indian spirituality better than any other scholar, writes about Vālmiki's work:

> The Ramayana is a work of the same essential kind as the Mahabharata; it differs only by a greater simplicity of plan, a more delicate ideal temperament and a finer glow of poetic warmth and colour. The main bulk of the poem in spite of much accretion is evidently by a single hand and has a less complex and more obvious unity of structure. There is less of the philosophic, more of the purely poetic mind, more of the artist, less of the builder.[27]

If the *Rāmāyaṇa* be compared to a superbly cut diamond, the *Mahābhārata* may be said to resemble a giant unpolished gem whose perfection and beauty lies in its very roughness and asymmetry. The character of the *Mahābhārata*, the 'Great [epic of the war] of the Bharata [-descendants]', is multilateral and thoroughly evasive. For it is, as Śrī Aurobindo asserts,

> not only the story of the Bharatas, the epic of an early event which had become a national tradition, but on a vast scale the epic of the soul and religious and ethical mind and social and political ideals and culture and life of India. It is said popularly of it and with a certain measure of truth that whatever is in India is in the Mahabharata. The Mahabharata is the creation and expression not of a single individual mind, but of the mind of a nation; it is the poem of itself written by a whole people.[28]

Aurobindo's remarks about this encyclopaedic epic of the Bhāratas are equally true of the *Gītā*. It is not so much the construction of an individual thinker with a bias for eclecticism, as the work of a genius who endeavoured, out of the very depths of his own being, to give expression to the potentialities of the whole Indian soul.

As is evident from the *Mahābhārata* itself (see I.1), the sage Vyāsa bequeathed the great epic in two compositions, a concise and a more elaborate version. Furthermore, it is stated in the same section that Vyāsa's original compilation comprised 24,000 verses and bore the title *Bharata*. He is also said to have written an epitome of 150 verses, *viz* the introduction to the *Mahābhārata*. Thereafter, the passage in question continues, he worked out a second version consisting of altogether six million stanzas, of which three million are known to the heavenly sphere (*deva-loka*), one and a half million to the sphere of the forefathers (*pitṛ-loka*), one million four hundred thousand to the genii (*gandharva*) and only a hundred thousand to the human world. The last-mentioned figure is justified by the form in which the epic is extant today.

The comprehensive material of the *Mahābhārata* is distributed over eighteen chapters. Although the plot of the *Gītā* can be understood on the basis of its own chapters, it may be useful to glance briefly at the contents of the chapters of the epic.

I. *ādi-parvan*

Leaving aside its practical function as an introduction to the whole of the epic, this chapter depicts the childhood and the career of the brothers Dhṛtarāṣṭra and Pāṇḍu. The blind king Dhṛtarāṣṭra had one hundred sons—the Kuru princes—who distinguished themselves by their bad character traits. Pāṇḍu, on the other hand, had five sons—the Pāṇḍavas—who were outstanding for their many moral excellences. Because of the premature death of Pāṇḍu, his five sons came under the care of Dhṛtarāṣṭra. Soon petty jealousies and quarrels developed between Dhṛtarāṣṭra's own sons and his protégés, which laid the foundation for the great war.

II. *sabhā-parvan*

Here a lively description is given of the assembly (*sabhā*) in Hastināpura, the capital of the Kuru land, where Yudhiṣṭhira, through a foul trick, lost his kingdom during a game of dice. The five Pāṇḍavas together with their wives and children were sent into exile for twelve years.

III. *vana-parvan*

This section describes the life in the forest (*vana*) of the banished sons of Pāṇḍu. It contains, among other outstanding pieces, the often translated story of Nala, who, like Yudhiṣṭhira, lost his kingdom through gambling. The legend of the faithful and devoted Savitrī is also related here.

IV. *virāṭa-parvan*

This is a description of the thirteenth year of exile which the five brothers were forced to spend incognito in the service of king Virāṭa.

V. *udyoga-parvan*

This part shows the preparations for the great civil war.

VI. *bhīṣma-parvan*

This section gives a meticulously detailed account of the first encounters on the battlefield. This chapter also contains the *Gītā* and receives its title from the chief defender of the Kurus, Bhīṣma, who was mortally wounded on the tenth day of the combat.

VII. *droṇa-parvan*

In this chapter the description of the minutes of the war is continued. Droṇa, who succeeded Bhīṣma, is killed.

VIII. *karṇa-parvan*

Karṇa, the new leader of the Kuru army, is similarly slain by the Pāṇḍavas.

IX. *śalya-parvan*

The war rages on. Among the Kurus Śalya and Duryodhana fall.

X. *sauptika-parvan*

The three surviving Kuru princes attack the encampment of the Pāṇḍavas at night and slaughter the whole army. Only the five brothers escape the carnage.

XI. *strī-parvan*

This chapter is a moving description of the funeral ceremonies of the survivors.

XII. *śānti-parvan*

Yudhiṣṭhira is crowned. Bhīṣma, who has delayed his death at will, relates the path to the attainment of emancipation. This chapter is considered one of the most important philosophical passages of the epic.

XIII. *anuśāsana-parvan*

Bhīṣma's didactic talk about law, morals and the value of ascetic practices is continued. And finally the great warrior and teacher passes away.

XIV. *aśvamedha-parvan*
Yudhiṣṭhira stages a colossal horse-sacrifice to consolidate his coronation.

XV. *āśramavasika-parvan*
The old king Dhṛtarāṣṭra withdraws into a forest hermitage (*āśrama*) and three years later loses his life in a conflagration.

XVI. *mausala-parvan*
This is an account of Kṛṣṇa's accidental death and his glorious ascension to heaven.

XVII. *mahāprasthānika-parvan*
Deeply shocked by Kṛṣṇa's death, the five sons of Pāṇḍu renounce their kingdom.

XVIII. *svargārohaṇika-parvan*
The five brothers, who in truth are divine beings, ascend to heaven.

To these eighteen books was appended in the third/fourth century A.D. the *Harivaṃśa* in which Kṛṣṇa's birth and youth is narrated in great detail. This supplement, comprising about 16,000 stanzas, has served later generations of Kṛṣṇa devotees as a prototype for other, more elaborate Kṛṣṇa biographies.

V. THE HISTORICAL SETTING

The *Mahābhārata* is a vast, ingenious and boldly constructed edifice whose epic kernel, the enmity between the sons of Pāṇḍu and the Kurus, is hidden—rather like the inmost doll of the well-known Russian doll-game—beneath a bulky mass of secondary narratives, minor episodes, religious discourses, and philosophical, cosmogonic and theological reflections. The actual nucleus of the epic consists of little more than 20,000 verses, that is about one-fifth of the total mass of the epic, and the rest reads like footnotes or appendices.

Academics have in the past tended to evaluate the *Gītā* as an interesting but not particularly indispensable footnote. There is little justification in this derogatory view. The contention that it is highly improbable that Kṛṣṇa should have initiated Arjuna into the secrets of his Yoga by holding a lengthy discourse just before the battle, fails to recognise the fact that the epic is in the first place a *spiritual* 'history', and the account of the conflict between two ancient tribes being of secondary importance. When looked at exclusively from the latter point of view there is little in the epic that makes sense or is palpable. On the other hand, the reader who leaves aside the question of historical validity and concerns himself with the spiritual content of the *Mahābhārata* will soon be convinced that Vyāsa was not so much recording objective history, but a-historic realities clothed either in symbols and myths or in the language of philosophy. The *Gītā* cannot be divorced from the main theme of the epic. On the contrary, it contains, as it were, the *raison d'être* for the war, not its historical reason but its spiritual justification.

The *external* circumstances leading to the grand battle and stripped of all unnecessary details, are the following: After the premature death of Pāṇḍu, the king of the Bhāratas, his blind brother Dhṛtarāṣṭra ascended the throne. There was an immediate enmity between the hundred sons of Dhṛtarāṣṭra and the five orphaned children of Pāṇḍu.[29] As they grew up the jealousies and quarrels deepened into solid hatred on the part of the hundred sons. When Yudhiṣṭhira, the oldest of the five brothers, was proclaimed heir-apparent on account of his distinction as a soldier, Dhṛtarāṣṭra's own children decided to rid themselves of their unwanted cousins. But their murderous assault miscarried. The five Pāṇḍavas fled into the forest and roamed the country disguised as *brāhmaṇas*.

One day they heard that Drupada, the ruler of the Pañcālas, intended to give away his daughter in marriage and that all noblemen of the North were invited to the festivities. They decided to go. King Drupada announced that he would give his daughter to that suitor who could hit a distant target through a high-mounted revolving ring with an immense bow he himself had made. Fate willed it that Arjuna of all contenders should accomplish this task and win the hand of the princess. At this contest the sons of Pāṇḍu also met Kṛṣṇa, leader of the Yādavas, who from then on became their inseparable friend and counsellor. The unexpected alliance with the kingdom of the Pāñcālas and the Yādava clan qualified the Pāṇḍavas to return to their homeland and renewedly claim their share of the paternal kingdom.

Dhṛtarāṣṭra agreed to parcel out the Kuru land, and the descendants of Pāṇḍu were allocated the country along the river Jumnā whereas the sons of the blind king kept the stretch of land along the Ganges. The sons of Pāṇḍu ruled wisely, and their dominion prospered. However, the happiness of the Pāṇḍavas was not intended to last for long. Yudhiṣṭhira, who, like most noblemen of his time, was a passionate dice player, soon brought ruin to the newly-founded dynasty. Being cleverly cheated by Śakuni, an uncle of Duryodhana the oldest son of Dhṛtarāṣṭra who had become jealous of his cousins' success, Yudhiṣṭhira lost his whole kingdom, including the possessions of his brothers. Only by the intervention of the old king were they able to escape enslavement. Instead they were sent into exile for thirteen long years of which they had to spend the last year incognito.

After the period of twelve years, which had been full of remarkable adventures, they went to the court of the Matsya king Virāṭa, and remained in his service under assumed names.

As soon as the thirteenth year had elapsed the Pāṇḍavas demanded the restoration of their kingdom. However, the hateful and power-mad Duryodhana rejected their plea. Kṛṣṇa, the head of the Yādavas, tried to negotiate between both parties, but his intercession remained fruitless. Finally, only one solution was left—war. As leaders of the two military forces, Arjuna and Duryodhana independently approached Kṛṣṇa for his support. Kṛṣṇa himself refused to fight, but gave them a choice between his powerful army and his council. Duryodhana decided for Kṛṣṇa's massive troops, whereas Arjuna was keen to secure Kṛṣṇa's personal aid. This is the situation as we find it at the outset of the *Gītā*, when the two clans confront each other on the *kuru-kṣetra*, the 'field of the Kurus'.

VI. THE *DRAMATIS PERSONAE* OF THE GĪTĀ

The teachings of the *Gītā* are cast into the form of a dialogue between the hierophany of the Supreme Reality, Kṛṣṇa, and the hero-yogin Arjuna, which is narrated by Saṃjaya to the aged monarch Dhṛtarāṣṭra. Thus merely four figures are involved. This quartet has often been endowed with a deeper esoteric significance. A symbolic correlation was thought to exist between Arjuna, Saṃjaya and Dhṛtarāṣṭra and the three primary-constituents of Nature, the *guṇas*, on the one hand, and Kṛṣṇa and the Primordial Ground of existence, the *nirguṇa-brahman*, on the other hand. This interpretation, strange and far-fetched as it may seem, proves quite valuable in explaining both the character of the *dramatis personae* of the *Gītā* and the nature of the *guṇas*. Their juxtaposition leads to mutual elucidation.

According to the ontological conception of the Sāṃkhya school of thought, on which the metaphysical notions of the *Gītā* are founded, the cosmos is like a web of unimaginable immensity woven by the incessant interaction of three primary forces, the *guṇas* (lit. 'strands'). Everything manifest, from the stupendous clusters of stars down to the infinitely minute particles of matter including the psycho-mental apparatus of man, is compounded of these quality-forces. Each *guṇa* has a distinct character. *Tamas* manifests itself in the power of inertia (on the cosmic scale), or in indolence and sloth (on the microcosmic or psychic scale). Its nuclear equivalent is the proton. *Rajas* represents the principle of activity—as symbolised by the electron. *Sattva* is of the nature of translucency, and it corresponds with the neutron. Beyond the realm of the *guṇas*, transcending the space-time universe, abides the Imperishable Reality.

Applied to our text, Kṛṣṇa as the source and support of the *Gītā* is the Reality beyond phenomenal existence. He is the One without a second (*ekam-advitīyam*), the Being devoid of the world-qualities.

Saṃjaya, blessed with divine vision, embodies the illuminating-uplifting quality of *sattva*.

Arjuna, again, is the impersonation of the principle of restless activity or *rajas*. Like Hamlet, he is ever doubting, arguing and vacillating.

Finally Dhṛtarāṣṭra represents *tamas*, the binding and veiling power in the universe and in the heart of man. Before the combat, Kṛṣṇa had offered Dhṛtarāṣṭra the restoration of his eye-sight so that he might follow for himself the development of the battle; but the old monarch, true to his spiritual blindness, preferred to remain enveloped in darkness. Thereupon Kṛṣṇa bestowed on Saṃjaya, the king's charioteer, the power to behold everything and to report it accurately while he himself remained immune. The word *saṃjaya* means 'victorious', and it is indicative of that victory (*jaya*) which Saṃjaya achieved over his mind thanks to the grace of Kṛṣṇa. For only a tranquil mind is competent to witness the eternal dialogue between the Divine (Kṛṣṇa) and the human soul (Arjuna).

Although Dhṛtarāṣṭra and Saṃjaya are indispensable elements in the *Gītā*, the centre of gravity in the drama lies in the dynamic relationship between Kṛṣṇa, the god-man, and Arjuna, the hero of divine birth. Before I proceed to delineate the deeper symbolical significance of these two prominent figures, I shall give a brief run-down of the historical facts related to Kṛṣṇa. About the 'historical' Arjuna, unfortunately, nothing definite can be said; in view of the fact that the *Mahābhārata* evinces an astoundingly consistent symbolism, it is not even certain whether Arjuna has any reality at all, or whether he is not simply a symbolic figure invented by Vyāsa.

But who was Kṛṣṇa?—Probably the earliest mention of a

seer-bard by that name is to be found in the *Ṛgveda* (VIII.74), which also refers to a monster called Kṛṣṇa (VIII.85. 13–15). A reference which is thought more likely to pertain to the epic Kṛṣṇa is contained in the *Chāndogya-Upaniṣad* (XXX.6). There Kṛṣṇa is called the son of Devakī and the pupil of Ghora Aṅgirasa, a sun-priest belonging to the tradition of the *Atharvaveda*. That there exists a certain connection between the epic Kṛṣṇa with the Aṅgirasa lineage is also hinted at by the *Gītā*, when Kṛṣṇa says of himself: 'Of the great seers I am Bhṛgu' (X.25). This sage stood in close relationship to the Aṅgirasas and the *Atharvaveda*, which originally was called *Atharva-Aṅgirasa-Saṃhitā*.

S. Radhakrishnan discovered a 'great similarity between the teaching of Ghora Aṅgirasa . . . and that of Kṛṣṇa in the *Gītā*'.[30] The thoughts of both teachers centre around the concept of sacrifice (*yajña*). But whereas Ghora Aṅgirasa is concerned with a spiritual interpretation of the priestly remuneration (*dakṣiṇā*), Kṛṣṇa's mind is rapt in the much wider problem of renunciation *in* action. Ghora Aṅgirasa merely states:

Asceticism, charity, uprightness, non-hurting and truthfulness—these [ought to be] one's remuneration [to the teacher].[31]

Kṛṣṇa, however, affirms:

Whatever you do, whatever you eat, whatever you offer, whatever you give, whatever asceticism you perform—do that, O son of Kuntī [= Arjuna], as an offering (*arpaṇa*) to Me. (IX.27)

Ghora Aṅgirasa's doctrine contains, as has been pointed out correctly, another feature for which there is a remarkable parallel in the *Gītā*. He refers to the yogic notion that the last thought in a man's life determines the form and quality of his state of being in the hereafter. His exact words are:

In the last hour (*anta-velāyām*) one should take refuge to these three [Vedic *mantras*]: 'You are the Imperishable, you are the Unshakable, you are the very essence of life (*prāṇa*).[32]

The *Gītā* devotes a whole chapter to this theme, and yet this correspondence does not really carry enough weight to establish the identity of the pupil of Ghora Aṅgirasa with the Kṛṣṇa of the epic. However, it is best to postpone a final decision on this point until further evidence is forthcoming.

The *Mahābhārata* contains several other references pertinent to Kṛṣṇa's tribal extraction and personality, but these do not add much to our picture of the 'historical' Kṛṣṇa. Let it suffice to say that he was a leader of the branch of an ancient Vedic tribe, the Yādavas.

Of greater importance is the fact that in the *Mahābhārata* and particularly in the *Gītā*, Kṛṣṇa is identified with the Ultimate Reality. In one verse his dual nature, as God and as man, is distinctly referred to:

The ignorant disregard Me, having a human body, not knowing Me as the Supreme Being, as the Great Lord of all things. (IX.11)

Kṛṣṇa is deemed a 'total incarnation' or *pūrṇa-avatāra* of the Divine, or, as the epic states elsewhere, a 'manifestation' (*pradūrbhāva*) of Viṣṇu. (However, in the *Viṣṇu-Purāṇa*, V.1.3[b], he is called a 'fraction of a fraction' of Viṣṇu.) He is the son of Vasudeva and Devakī, representing Heaven and Earth respectively. He is God in the shape of a human being. His life-story, particularly as depicted in the *Harivaṃśa* and the *Bhāgavata-Purāṇa*, is entirely that of a solar deity: Kṛṣṇa was born in a miraculous manner, he lived in seclusion in his youth, fought and won numerous fights with demons and other twilight creatures, had relations with several women, was persecuted, died a violent death and ascended into heaven. All solar deities are redeemers and upholders of the cosmic order. In his function as saviour, Viṣṇu the Supreme Being is taught to project Himself, in a suitable shape (not necessarily human), into the world wrought of space and time. Such projections are called *avatāras*, which literally means 'descents'.

Tradition gives three explanations for the name Kṛṣṇa. According to one interpretation, it means 'He who draws unto Him the hearts of His devotees'. The other esoteric etymology derives the name from *kṛṣī* ('earth' = existence) and *ṇa* (said to symbolise happiness) and thus links it with the being-bliss (*sad-ānanda*) of the Divine. Last, the most common explanation is that Kṛṣṇa means 'black one'. This reading carries a profound symbolic significance. For, the name Arjuna actually means 'White one'. Thus the two active agents of the Song Divine are symbolised by contrasting colours. This is a fascinating allusion to the contrary-complementary nature of Kṛṣṇa and Arjuna. Apparently different, they are essentially the same.

This is the undivided assumption throughout the epic. One passage brings it out quite clearly: Kṛṣṇa and Arjuna are no one else than Nārāyaṇa and Nara of old.[33] Legend knows that Nārāyaṇa and Nara together meditated in a golden chariot where they could not be seen by any mortal except for those who had obtained their special favour.[34] They are twin-souls, like Gilgamesh and Enkidu in the Babylonian mythology. This essential identity-in-duality is beautifully and perfectly expressed in the colour symbolism. Kṛṣṇa (*black*) is the absorption of all colours or qualities—he is the Signless One devoid of all qualities (*nir-guṇa*). And Arjuna (*white*) is the simultaneous presence of all colours and qualities (*sa-guṇa*)—that which bears sign. Between the infinity of the Black and the White stretches the narrow belt of the particularised, i.e. the empirical, universe. Kṛṣṇa is Viṣṇu, the beginning and the end of all manifestation. He says of himself: 'I am Time, the cause of world-destruction.' (XI.32)

It is because of this essential identity that Kṛṣṇa is able to reveal himself in his true nature to Arjuna in the eleventh chapter of the *Gītā*, and why Arjuna is able to perceive and withstand the grand transfiguration of Kṛṣṇa. Perhaps it is not incidental at all that one of the ten epithets of Arjuna is Kṛṣṇa.

It has been argued that the epithet 'black one' can hardly be aligned with Kṛṣṇa's solar character. Yet, is not the sun itself not only the life-giver and invigorator but also the death-bringer? Like the bloodthirsty goddess Kālī—the symbol of all-devouring Time—Viṣṇu (= Kṛṣṇa) is always depicted by iconography with a black hue. Besides, the mystic tradition knows also of a black aspect of the sun, which is visible only to the initiate.[35]

VII. PRINCIPLES OF INTERPRETATION

The first translation of the *Gītā* into a modern European language was prepared as long ago as the year 1785. This rendering, by Charles Wilkins, initiated a long series of attempts to make the *Gītā*, the Bible of Hinduism, accessible to the Western world. According to the Gita Press in Gorakhpur (Northern India), the *Gitā* is available today in more than thirty languages and at least a thousand individual editions. It ranks among the world's best-selling books.

Any translation is necessarily at the same time an interpretation. The various renderings of the *Gītā*, differing as they do from each other often quite considerably, are ample proof of this. These divergencies can be traced back to several sources. They are founded, on the one hand, in the complexity of the material itself and, on the other, in the linguistic abilities of the translator as well as in his variable capacity for comprehension, and, above all, empathy. A translation always involves the highly creative act of re-creating mentally, as far as possible, the original intellectual and emotional situation of the author.

In the case of works on abstract problems, this is by no means a simple task, even when the translator happens to be personally acquainted with the author. But it becomes an almost impossible task when the text is separated in time from the interpreter by more than two millennia. There arises the question not only of comprehending the symbols of an archaic language, but also of coming to terms with an altogether different style of thinking. The latter fact has rarely been taken into consideration by modern translators. It is not really surprising that the outcome of their efforts is none too impressive. Fortunately enough, scholars are beginning to realise that a purely philological and antiquarian treatment of texts like the *Gītā* cannot do justice to their true content, and a more adequate, 'contextual' approach to the study of these scriptures is gaining headway.

Nevertheless, philology and the historical disciplines are instrumental factors in understanding both the archaic language medium in which the *Gītā* was transmitted, and also in re-creating the intellectual *milieu* in which it was composed. However, the custom among indologists to employ these tools as ends in themselves compels strong criticism. The situation in Indology is very similar to that of Egyptology and kindred branches of knowledge. Over-anxious to remain within the officially accepted boundaries of 'scientific' research, these disciplines concentrate on what one might call the quantitative side of their subjects of study—words, dates, development of ideas—but neglect to a large measure the qualitative aspect, namely the *spirit* of the letter. The basic failure of the orthodox standpoint lies in the attempt to read the archaic *chiffres* along logical lines instead of applying the medium of their 'inventors', *viz* symbolic thinking, or analogical relating or intuitive apprehension as the case may be.

With the exception of a few scholars, it has not yet been fully grasped that Indology could fulfil a special humane task in our time where we witness the most massive confrontation between East and West. The dry, academically stilted approach of contemporary Indology, with little interest in the inner meaning of its subject matter, becomes singularly apparent in the *Gītā* which is brimming with significance. The sterile antiquarian approach to the interpretation of the *Gītā* is a comparatively recent event, although it can be said to have been alarmingly foreshadowed by Śaṅkara's uncompromising scholastic escapades.

Considerably older than the rational-analytical exegesis of the indologist is the view that the *Mahābhārata*, including the *Gītā*, is a vast-scaled *symbolical* representation which admits only of an *allegorical* interpretation. This appears to be the traditional Indian standpoint, widely held among the learned and uneducated alike. According to this view the epic depicts the drama of the human soul and its eternal struggle between the divine and the daemonic forces, between Good and Evil, Right and Wrong—*dharma* and *adharma*. The great figures of the epic are believed to represent particular aspects of the human being. So Bhīma is identified with 'strength', Yuyudhāna with 'success', Dhṛtaketu with 'prosperity', Cekitāna with 'tranquillity', Kaśirāja with 'purity', and so on.

Even though the allegorical interpretation takes into account the symbolic significance of the epic which is crudely ignored by philological analysis, it is yet like the latter only another form of *rationalisation*. It merely replaces logical analysis by analogical abstraction. Both methods are absolutistic and reductive in that they endeavour to isolate particular elements from the whole organic structure of the epic and dissect and categorise them. However, whereas the scientific method is concerned with what might be styled the surface-impressions, i.e. the form given to the thought, the allegorical procedure cuts through to the deeper strata, i.e. the spirit of the letter, though in a somewhat hazardous manner.

A more congenial approach in dealing with the symbolic component of the epic would be to elucidate simply the symbolic elements without rationalising or allegorising them. Only in this way can the polar character of a symbol, its wholeness, be preserved. To explain a symbol always means to destroy it to a certain extent; just as the electrons of an electronic microscope interfere with, alter and break the homogeneity of the micro-structure under examination. The function of a symbol is to point beyond itself, 'to open up levels of reality which otherwise are closed, and to open up levels of the human mind of which we otherwise are not aware'.[36] By the elucidation of a symbol I mean a rendering transparent of the whole symbol as an invaluable mediator between the inadequate capacity of the mind and the incommunicable nature of that which transcends it.

VIII. THE SYMBOLISM OF THE EPIC

Scholars have, on the whole, shown a remarkable disinterest in the symbolism of the great epic of India. Considering that Hindu and Buddhist literature and iconography are generally admitted to be replete with a highly refined symbolism, this attitude strikes one as a serious fiasco. There can be no doubt whatsoever about the total suffusion of Hinduism with a thoroughly developed symbolism. There are, to mention but a few instances, the eye-catching evidence of the intricate erotic symbolism employed in Tantrism and in the Kṛṣṇa cult of medieval India, or, in a much earlier period, the perplexing sacrificial symbolism of the *Brāhmaṇas*, or, still earlier, the captivating ethereal symbolism of the Vedic seer-bards. Perhaps it is no exaggeration to assert that symbolism is the real language of Hinduism. I would even go further and say that the *Mahābhārata* may be regarded as the authoritative 'grammar' of that 'language'. Any open-minded perceptive reader, who cares to unseal the fusty and yellowed pages of this great book, will soon be convinced that the *Mahābhārata* is a creation of profound depth. As the epic itself points out:

Once upon a time the gods decided to weigh the five *Vedas* against each other. They placed the four Vedas on the one side of the scale, and the epic on the other. The scales lowered towards the side of the epic, because its mysteries weighed heavier than those of the four collections of the ancient sacred tradition taken together. From then on the epic was called the great epic of the Bhāratas.[37]

This is surely more than a mere attempt to establish the superiority of the epic over the ancient Vedic canon. Rather this story should be looked upon as a firm self-testimony of the epic's inherent spiritual and symbolic momentousness.

To what superlative degree the mind of the author of the *Mahābhārata* moved in the sphere of symbols becomes apparent with utmost clarity in the legend of Aṣṭāvakra and his protagonist Vandin. As this probably unique dispute is little known, I append a full translation of it. (*See Appendix I*)

Another conclusive illustration of the presence of an acute symbolic tendency in the *Mahābhārata* is the prominence given to the number 18.

Both the *Mahābhārata* and the *Gītā* consist of 18 divisions. The battle wages for exactly 18 days. The army of the sons of Pāṇḍu claims the support of 18 *mahārathas* or 'great warriors'; *mahāratha* is the title bestowed by the king on a loyal and heroic soldier who is capable of fighting ten thousand men all at once. The total military strength of both parties is 18 *akṣauhiṇīs*, seven on the Pāṇḍava side and eleven on the Kaurava. An *akṣauhiṇī* is defined as an army of 21,870 chariots, 21,870 elephants, 65,610 horses and 109,350 foot-soldiers. This is a total of 218,700 units. This figure can also be expressed as 18 × 12,150, and the total of the digit of this number is likewise 18.

Furthermore, Dhṛtarāṣṭra is said to have died 18 years after the battle on the *kuru-kṣetra*, and Kṛṣṇa passed away after the lapse of another 18 years. In the twelfth chapter of the epic, the 18 *guṇas* of *brahman* are mentioned. The second chapter mentions the 18 families of the Northern Bhojas (II.14.25) as well as the 18 clans of the Mādhavas. More instances could easily be cited. What seems most significant is the fact that this number 18 plays a similarly remarkable role in most other branches of Hindu literature, like grammar, poetry, cosmography, botany, medicine, law and philosophy, and it is also to be found in abundance in Buddhism and Jainism.[38]

The symbolic 'value' of the number 18 is not immediately apodictic. Indian pundits connect it with the concept of sacrifice (*yajña*), and there seems to be good reason for this. First of all, the numerical symbol 18 apparently involves the idea of 'completeness' or 'wholeness'—not as a static, uniform condition, but as a homogeneous yet multiform process. As such it may be taken to represent the cosmos as a continuous process of becoming.

Through self-immolation the Primeval Being created the manifold universe. This act of self-sacrifice is endlessly repeated by the Creator (Prajāpati)[39] and, in reversed order, by all beings in the cosmos; lower life-units become, involuntarily, the prey of higher life-units. In other words forms of existence of a lower order of organisation and complexity sustain the life of the more complex forms of existence by 'sacrificing' their individual lives. Hence to the Vedic seers 'sacrifice' became the 'hub of the world'. It is this idea which reappears in the enigmatic words of Kṛṣṇa:

Know that [all] activity arises from the Primal-Being [i.e. *brahma*]. The Primal-Being is born from the Imperishable (*akṣara*). Therefore, the omnipresent *brahman* is ever established in sacrifice. (III.15)

And:

I [Kṛṣṇa] am sacrifice. (IX.16)

Understood in this wider sense, sacrifice continues life. It ensures the wholeness of creation, the continuum of the Many-in-the-One. Sacrifice is thus synonymous with the cosmic order (*ṛta*). The ethics of the *Gītā* is based on exactly this fundamental insight into the sacrificial self-limitation of the Creator and the created. A modern variation of this ancient conception is to be met with in contemporary Ecology where, significantly enough, one speaks of a 'food chain'. Noteworthy here is the choice of terminology which is evidently borrowed from the vocabulary of the mythic structure of consciousness. An excerpt from the *Taittirīya-Upaniṣad* will bear this out:

The Primal-Being (*brahma*)[40] is food (*anna*). For truly, beings here in the world are born from food. When born they live by food. On dying they enter into food.[41]

The same *Upaniṣad* contains a remarkable passage in which verbal expression is given, in the form of a chant, to a most exalted enstatic experience of the Cosmic Whole:

Oh, wonderful! Oh, wonderful! Oh, wonderful!
I am food. I am food. I am food.
I am food-eater. I am food-eater. I am food-eater.
I am unity-maker. I am unity-maker. I am unity-maker.
I am the first-born of the world-order (*ṛta*),
Prior to the gods, in the navel of immortality.
He who gives me away, he indeed preserves me.
I, [who am] food, eat the eater of food.
I have overcome the whole world![42]

Life means sacrifice. The *Bṛhadāraṇyaka-Upaniṣad* (I.1) likens the world to a sacrificial horse (*aśva*) and the process of world-creation to the horse-sacrifice (*aśva-medha*) which was widely practised in ancient India. What is true of the cosmos as a whole is no less true of its multitudinous constituent forms. As the *Chāndogya-Upaniṣad* (III.16.1) puts it pithily:

Man, verily, is sacrifice.

This brings to mind an ambiguous passage in the *Muṇḍaka-Upaniṣad* which speaks of 18 'sacrificial forms' (*yajña-rūpa*). These are ordinarily understood to refer to the participants in a sacrifice: the 16 priests together with the sacrificer and his wife. As we have seen, the upaniṣadic seers identified, by way of analogy, sacrifice with man, and therefore it is quite permissible to locate those 18 'sacrificial forms' *within* man. However, since the *Upaniṣads* only know of a sixteenfold division of man, we are forced to look for an explanation of these 18 'forms' elsewhere in literature. Significantly, a persuasive answer is supplied by the *Mahābhārata*—thus completing our investigation into the symbolism of the number 18:

The [fourteen] 'instruments'[43] and the [three] 'states'[44] are considered the seventeen qualities [of the corporeal human being]. [In addition to] these there is, as eighteenth [part] the 'embodied' [Self][45] which dwells in the body [and which] is eternal.[46]

Thus 18 appears to be the symbolic equivalent of 'man as sacrifice'. And this, it seems, is the keynote of the *Mahābhārata* and the *Gītā*.

ESSENTIAL DOCTRINES

1. THE REALITY BEYOND THE ONE AND THE MANY

This First which in Itself is and from which all things have been created is God.[1]

That God is present in space without space, and in time without time, is a consequence of His being always the same from eternity to eternity...Hence it follows that nature is separated from God, and yet He is omnipresent therein...[2]

These words of the Swedish seer and philosopher Emanuel Swedenborg epitomise beautifully and perfectly the metaphysical position of Kṛṣṇa. God is all that is, the visible and the invisible. He is the *Whole*. The Sanskrit writers employ the word *pūrṇa* or 'plenum' to express the inexhaustible fullness of the All-encompassing Reality. A famous invocation found at the beginning of various *Upaniṣads* reads:

The Whole is that. The Whole is this. From the Whole the Whole is derived. The Whole taken from the Whole, the Whole [still] remains.[3]

God is the one Supreme Reality, beyond which and outside which there is naught. It is worshipped under different names according to man's limited capacity of comprehension.

Even those who are devoted to other deities [and] worship them possessed of faith—[they] worship Me alone...(IX.23)

This Supreme Being is as much the Yahveh of the Pentateuch as It is the Allah of the pious Mohammedan, or the bloodthirsty deity Kālī of certain Hindu sects, or the Silent Ground of the Christian mystic Meister Eckehart. Kṛṣṇa who belongs to the Vaiṣṇava tradition designates It as *puruṣottama* or 'supreme person'. This smacks of anthropomorphism, but a closer look at the *Gītā* soon rectifies this impression. The reason for this choice in naming the Nameless lies in the fact that Kṛṣṇa endeavours to give weight to an important and previously much neglected aspect of the transcendental 'situation' of Selfhood, namely the inner relation existing between the Whole and the awakened or integrated Self, that is, between God and the emancipated entity who has recovered his original essential oneness with the Uncreate Ground. This relationship beyond space and time is one of ever-flowing love (*bhakti*). This point will be elaborated at a later stage.

It is to the sophist Protagoras that we trace back the well-known phrase 'Man is the measure of all things'. This haughty formulation is the result of Protagoras' blatant denial of the existence of anything that was not registered by the senses and capable of being taken in by the ordinary mind. His subjectivism and relativism were heavily criticised and attacked by Socrates and his pupil Plato. In fact, we owe to the latter the antithetical phrase 'God is the measure of all things'.[4] This is definitely the standpoint which Kṛṣṇa assumes. God is the ultimate limit, Himself unlimited, infinite and eternal.

The God spoken of in the *Gītā* is the living God of the Pāñcarātra-Vaiṣṇava movement. This movement is older than Buddhism and has its roots in the non-Vedic strata of the ancient Indian culture. The Pāñcarātra tradition has three outstanding characteristics which are in strong contrast to the orthodox Vedic tradition, with its seemingly absurd preoccupation with sacrificial rituals and its rather marked exclusivism.

Firstly, the Pāñcarātra introduced the monotheistic (*ekānta*) worship of God together with the inseparable attitude of devotion-love (*bhakti*) towards the Divine. This stood out against the hierarchy of impersonal divine forces (*deva*) of the Vedic pantheon. The early Vedic people believed in a multitude of deities to which they ascribed certain functions and allotted certain areas in nature. Gradually out of this Polytheism evolved both Monotheism and Monism. The main-stream took to the monistic conception of God. It was mainly this tradition against which the Pāñcarātra thinkers and seers had to defend and fortify their Monotheism.

A further decisive point on which they differed from the established religion was their introduction of the cultic worship of God in the temples and His depiction in pictorial form. In Brāhmaṇism, on the other hand, with its strict insistence on an impersonal, featureless and nameless Absolute, pictorial worship of God was totally absent. To this day, not a single image of *brahman* can be found; only one temple is consecrated to the Supreme Reality.

Finally, a third feature of the Pāñcarātra religion which deserves special mention is its astounding liberal-mindedness regarding women, caste, and foreigners. The brāhmaṇical orthodoxy took a rather severe, often derogatory attitude towards them, which even today has its unfortunate repercussions in India. The following verse of the *Gītā* is paradigmatic of the enlightened attitude of Vaiṣṇavism:

> Those, O son-of-Pṛthā, who take refuge in Me, though [they be] of sinful birth, women, merchants and even serfs—they [all] attain the supreme course (*gati*). (IX.32)

The Pāñcarātra religion, and its successor Vaiṣṇavism, injected new vitality into the fossilising Vedic culture and provided the people with a new practical philosophy which gave them a directive and a fresh interest in life.

Vaiṣṇavism thus balanced the highly abstract attitude towards God and the arid legalism of the brāhmaṇical establishment. At the same time it avoided falling prey to the imminent danger inherent in all monotheistic religions, namely to regard God as so exclusively transcendental and remote from his creation as to make it impossible for His worshippers to approach Him except with fear and absolute servility.

The religion or philosophy of Vaiṣṇavism can best be described as Pan-en-theism. This is the doctrine that all subsists in God, whilst He is not identical with, nor exhausted by, His creation. As Kṛṣṇa the incarnate Lord Himself affirms:

By Me, unmanifest in form, this entire [universe] was spread-out. All things abide in Me, but I do not subsist in them. (IX.4)

Elsewhere (VII.12) he says:

Moreover, know that those states (*bhāva*) of luminosity, dynamism and obscurity [proceed] from Me. Yet I am not in them, they are in Me.

In both stanzas Kṛṣṇa reveals His divine nature and authorship of the world. There is nothing which does not ultimately derive from Him or is sustained by Him. Himself imperishable and unmanifest, He comes into being by his self-power (*ātma-māyā*).[5] This eternal self-unfolding surpasses reason and can, at best, be intuited. It is a process which takes place within the Whole and therefore is only intelligible to the Whole, if one persists in operating with such relative terms at all.

For Śaṅkara, God's power of self-multiplication (*vibhāga-śakti*) is based on false knowledge (*mithyā-jñāna*). Kṛṣṇa is adamantly set against this point of view, which, in the last analysis, advocates an attitude of belittlement of life. He vouches that God, the Whole, is replete with powers which are definitely not illusory. Śaṅkara's world-view appears imperfect. He affirms the reality of the One only, denying the independent existence of the Many. For him the appearance of the manifold universe rests entirely on a misconception or delusion (*abhimāna*). Hence individuality is also reduced to being a mere phantom (*ābhāsa*). Of course, Śaṅkara also failed to account satisfactorily for his concept of delusion which renders all plurality illusory. There is not a trace of doubt in Kṛṣṇa's mind that this world of multiplicity is real. It is true, though, that Śaṅkara rejected the idea promulgated by some schools of Buddhist Idealism that the world is only a product of our imagination. But often enough he comes dangerously close to maintaining this extravagant notion. Kṛṣṇa, at any rate, regards the Many to be as real as the One. Because it is an aspect of the Whole which comprises both the One and the Many.

This conception has its prototype in the *Ṛgveda* where in

the 'Hymn of Man' (*puruṣa-sūkta*) the Supreme Being is extolled in terms similar to those employed in the *Gītā* and other Pāñcarātra scriptures.

1. Thousand-headed was the [Supreme] Man, thousand-eyed, thousand-footed. He embraced the earth on all sides, and stood beyond the breadth of ten fingers.
2. The [Supreme] Man is all this, that which was and which shall be. He is the Lord of immortality, which He grows beyond through [sacrificial] food.
3. Such is His greatness, and still greater than that is the [Supreme] Man. One-fourth of Him is all beings. The three-fourths of Him is the immortal in Heaven.
4. Three-fourths on high rose the [Supreme] Man. One-fourth of Him arose again here [in this world]. Hence in all directions He spread abroad, as that which eats and that which eats not.
5. From Him the Resplendent One (*virāj*)[6] was born, from the Resplendent One the *puruṣa*[7]. He when born reached beyond the earth behind as well as before.
6. When the gods spread out the sacrifice with the *puruṣa* as oblation, spring was its ghee, summer the fuel, autumn the oblation.
13. The moon was born from His mind (*manas*), from His eye was born the sun, from His mouth Indra and Agni, from His breath Vāyu was born.
14. From His navel arose the mid-region, from his head the Heaven originated, from His feet the earth, the quarters from His ear. Thus did they [i.e. the gods] fashion the worlds. (X.90)

Here the primeval giant, the *puruṣa*, also encountered in the mythologies of other countries, is sacrificed by the gods who fashion out of the members of his body all the many existing things. This archetypal sacrifice later came to be understood as a self-slaughtering of the Supreme Being who splits Himself into incalculable fragments thus creating the universe and man. In the *Gītā*, this self-immolation does not mean the death of the Primeval One. The creation of the Many out of the One does not imply the negation of the unity of the One. The world-creation does not rend asunder the original wholeness of the Whole. On the contrary, it is an essential aspect of this all-containing wholeness. Not being a technical treatise on philosophy, the *Gītā* does not elaborate this point beyond the bare essentials. This was the task of Rāmānuja who was preoccupied with the question of the relationship between the One and the Many.

A fitting exemplification of Kṛṣṇa's particular standpoint is found in the *Śvetāśvatara-Upaniṣad* which, in a way, is for Śaivaism what the *Gītā* is for Vaiṣṇavism. The text in question reads (IV.1[a]):

> The One who, [Himself] without colour, by the multiple application of power (*śakti-yoga*), shares out innumerable colours (according to His] hidden motive...

The *Gītā* itself contains the following beautiful stanzas:

> 15. [That] is without and within all beings, unmoving and yet moving. That cannot be known because of [Its] subtleness. That is far-standing [and] yet near.
> 16. And undivided (*avibhakta*), It abides in beings seeming divided (*vibhakta*). That is to be known as the support-of-beings, (their) devourer and (their) generator. (XIII.15–16)

These verses remind one of another ancient *Upaniṣad* which, together with the *Kaṭha-* and *Śvetāśvatara-Upaniṣad*, overtops the great mass of monistic writings by its sublime theism which resembles that of the *Gītā*. This is the *Īśa-Upaniṣad* which is the shortest and perhaps the most expressive and enchanting text of this entire genre of gnostic literature. This merits partial translation at least.

1. Whatever moves in the world
—all this cast upon the Lord.[8]
Rejoice in this renunciation
and do not covet anyone's wealth.

2. Even doing deeds here [on earth],
One may desire to live a hundred years.
Thus is it with you, not otherwise.
The deed does not defile a man.

3. Daemonic, verily, are those worlds,
covered with blind darkness.
To them, at death, go those people
who are slayers-of-the-Self.

5. It moves, It moves not.
It is far, and It is near.
It is within everything,
and It is outside of all this.

6. He who sees all beings in the Self
and the Self in all beings
—he no [longer] hates.

7. Recognising [Him] in whom the Self
became all beings
—what delusion is there, what sorrow
[for him who] sees the unity?

8. He, the all-pervader, bright, bodiless,
scatheless, sinewless, the pure,
unpierced by sin, the poet, thinker,
encompasser, self-existent,
has distributed the things according
to their nature for eternal times.

9. Those who worship nescience (*avidyā*)
enter into blind darkness.
Into apparently greater darkness [enter]
those who delight in knowledge (*vidyā*).

10. Other, they say, is [It] than knowledge.
Other, they say, is [It] than nescience.
Thus have we heard from the wise
who explained It to us.

11. He who knows both knowledge and nescience together
crosses over the death [of] nescience and
obtains the immortality-nectar [of] knowledge.

R. C. Zaehner sums up the theological position of the *Gītā* in the following words:

> God is the One: but He is not a One who obliterates and nullifies the manifold: rather He binds the many together in a coherent whole since the whole is his body and a body is an organism in which all the parts are interdependent.[9]

God is the 'unmanifest beyond the unmanifest', the 'supreme Self', the foundation of both the manifest world and its unmanifest core; and He is the abode of the conglomeration of Selves. Kṛṣṇa thus introduces the revolutionary idea that God is the base of even the imperishable substratum of all world-phenomena, the *brahman*, which the *Upaniṣads* equate with the Self (*ātman*) within man. There are several verses in the *Gītā* which bear out that the *yogin* 'having become *brahman*' (*brahma-bhūta*)[10] draws nearer the ultimate resting-place in God, by attaining unexcellable love (*bhakti*) for Kṛṣṇa the Lord. This is as clear a rejection of the upaniṣadic pantheistic trend as one can get. Kṛṣṇa does not deny the identity of the Self, as the apex of the human soul, with the world-ground (*brahman*). At the same time, however, he recognises that this is not the full truth. For, wherein does the identity of *ātman* and *brahman* subsist, if not in the Whole?

Kṛṣṇa mentions two 'natures' of God, a higher and a lower one. His higher nature consists of the collective transcendental Self-monads or units of consciousness for which the ambiguous term *jīva-bhūta* is employed in the *Gītā* (VII.5). Translated freely this means 'life-principle'. It is contrasted with the unmanifest core of the objective world, the lower nature of God which is also given the name *brahman* or world-ground. Both these natures or modes act as a receptacle of God's creative activity and jointly produce the phenomenal universe of subjects and objects. The many Selves and the world-ground represent the male and female principles respectively. Thus from the point of view of the finite, the Supreme Being appears to comprise the following triad:

(i) the conglomeration of transcendental Selves
(ii) the transcendental core of the world
(iii) the manifest world of space and time

God is present most essentially in the conscious Self-monads. His immanence in the human soul is, in fact, the real and fundamental concern of the religious and philosophical traditions of India. No mysticism would be possible without this presence of God in His creation, particularly in man's inmost centre of being. And mysticism is surely the essence of all forms of Indian philosophy.

Indian thought is in complete contrast with its modern Western counterpart. No Indian thinker would have ever remained satisfied with Wittgenstein's disheartening conclusion at the end of his famous *Tractatus Logico-Philosophicus*, where he bluntly states that even if philosophy could show the fly the way out of the bottle, it would be unable to actually help the fly to get out of it, 'because philosophy leaves everything where it is'. On the other hand in the East all philosophical achievements are regarded as meaningless and futile if they have no bearing on real life, if they cannot lift man out of the thicket of spiritual ignorance into the realm of a purer, more genuine and infinitely more worthwhile existence.

The observations of A. W. Watts are particularly relevant:

> If we look deeply into such ways of life as Buddhism and Taoism, Vedanta and Yoga, we do not find either philosophy or religion as these are understood in the West. We find something more nearly resembling psychotherapy...The main resemblance between these Eastern ways of life and Western psychotherapy is in the concern of both with bringing about changes of consciousness...[11]

The common denominator of Eastern and Western systems of directed introspection is that both try to achieve a transmutation of the ordinary awareness. However, in the East this involves a much more rigorous approach. Western psychotherapy is still very much a matter of the 'socialisation' of the individual, whereas in the East the primary interest is to bring a person 'to himself', or rather to guide him to a full

Self-awakening. The West is more concerned with the self than with the Self. Yet among the more advanced psychotherapists there is a slow but discernible shift towards the Self as the life-giving nucleus of the psycho-somatic organism. But on the whole, to most therapists and psychologists, the Self is still only a remote possibility, as God is to most philosophers.

Kṛṣṇa, on the other hand, does not theorise. He speaks with the certainty of experience. God and Self are to him unimpeachable realities. God indwells the human soul, and it is only by the turning inward of the mind that He can be realised as the immortal 'inner controller' (*antar-yāmin*). On this point there is a deep and instructive conversation between the sage Yājñavalkya and Uddālaka Āruṇi in the *Bṛhadāraṇyaka-Upaniṣad* (III.8.1–23); these are the most pertinent verses:

16. He who abiding in the vital-force (*prāṇa*) is [yet] other than the vital-force, whom the vital-force does not know, whose body is the vital-force, who controls the vital-force from within—He is the Self, the Inner Controller, the Immortal.
17. He who abiding in speech is [yet] other than speech, whom speech does not know, whose body is speech, who controls speech from within—He is the Self, the Inner Controller, the Immortal.

The same formula is repeated with regard to eye, ear, skin, knowledge and seed. The passage is concluded with this verse:

23. [He is] the unseen Seer, the unheard Hearer, the unthought Thinker, the unknown Knower—other than He there is no seer, other than He there is no hearer, other than He there is no thinker, other than He there is no knower. He is the Self, the Inner Controller, the Immortal.

Although Kṛṣṇa does not adopt the expression 'inner controller' for the Self, he fully accepts the idea implied in it. God is the only real agent in the drama of the world. He guides the lives of men. By his ordinance (*adhyakṣa*) the world-ground issues forth the manifold universe. In the form of the Self, God is either man's 'friend' or 'foe', depending on whether or not the desire-nature, the 'lower' self, has been subdued.

Kṛṣṇa himself is the living proof of God's immanence. As a total incarnation of the Divine, he gives testimony to God's eternal presence in the realm of conditioned existence. Kṛṣṇa symbolises the Self in every sentient being.

It is because of the indwelling of the Supreme Being in man's soul that he is *capax Dei*. Meister Eckehart never tired of speaking of the ground of the soul, the *bürgelin* ('citadel'), which God alone can touch. In this purest and noblest part of the soul the 'birth of Christ' is consummated. There God's Word sounds eternally and without obstruction. It is that uncreate centre of illumination in which is born true gnosis (*jñāna*) and from which the divine light flows out into all parts of mind and body.

Kṛṣṇa is quite clear on one point: It is God's grace (*prasāda*) or compassion (*anukampā*) which causes this illumination and upliftment of the human being. All man can do is to empty himself more and more so as to make room for the fullness of the Supreme Being. Yet this grace is not that which a benign sovereign might display towards his subjects. It is not a matter of personal preference, and therefore it can also not be obtained surreptitiously. God thwarts all opportunism by His sheer indifference.

> I am the same in all beings. To Me there is none hateful or dear. But those who worship me with love (*bhakti*), they are in Me and I am in them. (IX.29)

Thus God's grace is not an isolated occurrence, but an impersonal *omniactive* force which draws nearer to the Divine Source all those who have purified and raised the self by the Self. The conception of God as saviour, in this sense, is not incompatible with the simultaneous affirmation of His supreme aloofness. In God all opposites coincide. He is, as the sage Vaiśampāyana expressed it, 'non-doer and doer at the same time, effect as well as cause'.[12] Without God's indwelling in the world, there could be no elevating grace. Buddhism which denies the immanence of the Supreme Reality consequently does not admit the existence of a universal force which uplifts and ennobles those who are prepared for it. On this issue the *Bhagavad-Gītā* is unanimous with the *New Testament*:

He who abides in Me, and I in him, the same brings forth much fruit; for without Me you can do nothing. (John XV.5)

It would be quite wrong to assume that man is totally at the mercy of the whims of an ineffable power. Man as an emanation of the Supreme Reality is not completely dependent and powerless, nor is God erratic in His conferment of grace. He releases those souls who are irrevocably turned towards Him, from the fetters of His 'lower nature', and draws them into the unclouded light of His immortal presence. Those whose hearts are set on finite things and ephemeral pleasures, He fastens tighter to the ever-turning wheel of time.

Once again it is the Christian Meister Eckehart who faithfully echoes what Kṛṣṇa preached long before Christ:

I shall never thank God that He loves me, for He cannot do otherwise, whether He wills to or not: His nature constrains Him to it. Yet I shall thank Him that in His goodness He cannot but love me.[13]

This sublime yet matter-of-fact attitude, characteristic of most advanced forms of enlightened mysticism, never exercised sufficient force or lasting influence on the wider mass of religious-minded people. It remained, rather, the prerogative of those few who were intellectually well-equipped. The period following Eckehart and his immediate disciples bears this out.

So also does the development of Vaiṣṇavism subsequent to the *Gītā*. The ideals of love (*bhakti*) and grace (*prasāda*) came to the fore and gradually developed to such an extreme that man was compared to a helpless kitten completely dependent on the mother-cat. For instance, the *āḷvārs*, the ancient Vaiṣṇava saints of South India, insisted that God's grace was a spontaneous act which did not rest on the effort or the merit of the worshipper. In other religious circles, the loving participation (*bhakti*) between God and man and *vice versa*, which Kṛṣṇa exalted, was changed into a full-fledged erotic mysticism with strong emotional overtones and which, at times, gave way to brute eroticism. The Mahārāj sect was notorious for its moral degeneracy, and in modern times it is the *holī* festival, celebrated in certain regions of Northern India, which attracts our attention because of its pronounced Dionysian quality, combining as it does religious fervour with institutionalised acts of obscenity and aggression.

But these excesses do not encroach on the clear vision of Kṛṣṇa which had a superb 'levelling' influence on the development of the cultural life of India. Whatever enervations and distortions his teaching may have suffered in later times, they were definitely not rooted in any shortcoming intrinsic to the gospel itself, but were the direct outcome of the natural weakness and susceptibility of man.

II. THE SELF: CREATIVE CENTRE OF THE HUMAN PERSONALITY

The philosophy of the *Gītā* is the product of many centuries of intensive reflection on the Why and Whence of things. From earliest times Indian man has shown a distinct predilection for philosophical speculation about the nature of man and the universe. Long before the rise of Greek thought, he grappled with the profoundest problems of philosophy. By the time the *Gītā* was compiled, philosophical enquiry had already reached a noteworthy degree of maturity, complexity and coherence. The musings of the early Vedic seers had developed in depth and breadth as well as in clarity and precision. What was revealed to them in synthetic visions was distilled from the language of poetry and mythology and crystallised into world-views (*darśana*) of varied homogeneity.

In the *Gītā* three great philosophical trends are discernible. These are Vedānta, Sāṃkhya and Yoga. To simplify one may say that the Non-dualism of Vedānta constitutes the overall metaphysical fundation of the doctrine of Kṛṣṇa, whilst the Sāṃkhya supplies the cosmological and metapsychological framework and Yoga the ethical substance. However, this ought not to give the impression that the doctrine of Kṛṣṇa is an incongruous patchwork of these three different schools of thought—a view which is all too often implied in the assumption that the author of the *Gītā* was an eclectic. The teachings of Kṛṣṇa are, as will be shown, an organic and coherent structure in which all component parts are meaningfully related to each other. It is not simply a philosophy of compromise, but a true synthesis and reconciliation. It synchronises the upaniṣadic conception of the 'Absolute devoid of qualities' (*nirguṇa-*

brahman) with the theistic teachings of the Epics and the *Purāṇas*.

In conformity with the upaniṣadic tradition, the *Gītā* declares that there is one self-same Being, for which it proposes various appellations, such as Puruṣottama, Primeval God, Supreme Abode or Eternal Puruṣa. However, this Being is not identical with the transcendent Single Being of Advaita-Vedānta which is held to be inactive, without parts and uncreate and which appears to be many only on account of nescience (*avidyā*). According to this view the phenomenal world is merely a 'quivering of the mind' (*citta-spandita*), whereby the mind is considered synonymous with the transcendent pure subject, the *ātman*.[14] The universe is compared to an imaginary castle in the sky, or to a dream or hallucination. The Manifold is illusory. There is only the One. This notion is antipodal to the radical pluralism and functionalism of Theravāda-Buddhism which obstinately denies an ultimate reality underlying the multiplicity of phenomena and sees everywhere and in everything only perpetual becoming or process.

Kṛṣṇa assumes a mediating position. Being, to him, is wholly transcendent as well as wholly immanent, eternal and infinite as well as temporal and finite. It is the visible and the invisible, one and many, or rather one in many and many in one. The world-process is by no means illusory (*māyika*), but indisputably real. Creation is an actual transformation within the infinitude of the Whole. This is Pan-en-theism: all is in God. The *Gītā* compares the cosmos to a giant tree which has its roots 'above', i.e. in the transcendent One, and its branches 'below', i.e. in the phenomenal world.[15] Its essential form, however, is not visible to the human eye; neither is its beginning and its end. The finite mind is unable to ascertain the reason for the existence of the contingent universe, as it is totally incapable of comprehending the essential nature of the Whole. It cannot reach beyond itself. Therefore no logic can prove or disprove the reality of the Ultimate Being.

However, it can be subjectively verified in spontaneous 'intimations of Being' (*Seinsfühlungen*),[16] that is, at moments of openness towards Being, when our every-day perceptual and conceptual activity is temporarily suspended. Full verification takes place in the direct realisation of Being, when man discovers or rather recovers the ground of his own being and thereby finds himself absorbed in the wholeness of the Ultimate Being. Martin Heidegger, one of the most creative thinkers of our age, expressed this fact in an inspiring metaphor. He likened Being to a forest and man's relationship to Being to that of a clearing in the forest: Only in man can Being show itself, because it is man who can assume an attitude of creative distance towards himself and towards his environment.

Since Being itself eludes the human mind, man has to content himself with the apprehension of the phenomenal realities, the Manifold. Probably the first more elaborate analysis of the world-process is that of the Sāṃkhya school which, in a sense, anticipated the intentional-analytical method of modern Phenomenology. The ontological model of the structure of the world as advocated by the Sāṃkhya philosophers is not the product of pure ratiocination. Rather it has grown out of intuitive ideation and, one may reasonably assume, deeper visions in states of intensified awareness as achieved through yogic techniques. The latter conjecture seems to be particularly warranted by the fact that the early Sāṃkhya schools were most intimately associated with the Yoga movement, which emphasised the voluntary and controlled 'heightening' of consciousness.

It seems that it was only when the Sāṃkhya thinkers began to discard the well-tried methods of Yoga and relied more and more on reasoning alone that their phenomenological insights into the world-structure assumed the form of an inflexible, 'closed' and hence non-viable system. The *Sāṃkhya-Kārikā* of Īśvara Kṛṣṇa, probably written in the second century A.D., is a characteristic and deterrent example for this fallacious and barren development. On the other hand, the original creative impetus of the epic Sāṃkhya theory was kept alive in those schools which remained in close proximity to the yogic movement in which the continued practical-meditative 'sounding out' of the diverse modes of existence and the ever revitalising direct encounter with Being prevented, to a large extent, the construction of rigid metaphysical systems. A fitting example of this practice-orientated approach is the Sāṃkhya-based ontology of the *Yoga-Sūtra* of Patañjali, the *vade-mecum* of Classical Yoga.

This brings us to the ontological 'map' propounded in the *Gītā*. The use of the word 'map' calls for an explanation. In contrast with modern Western thinkers who tend to be addicted to the acquisition of knowledge purely for the sake of knowledge, the Indian philosophers, by and large, pursue knowledge for the express purpose of enriching human life. In fact, the knowledge they are seeking has to be of practical utility in the exploration of the 'spiritual dimension' of the universe. Only knowledge which, ultimately, has the power to conduce to the realisation of the Essence of all things, the attainment of spiritual emancipation (*mokṣa*), is considered a worthy object of philosophical inquiry. Hence in India and in the East in general, philosophy functions as a way of life. It is *theoría*: vision-based organic knowledge, as opposed to reasoned-out theory.

To be genuinely fruitful and valuable knowledge has to grow into unmediated experience. The Indian philosopher is never satisfied with a purely intellectual knowledge of the world-phenomena; his search penetrates far beyond this: he wants to *experience* and, indeed, inwardly identify with the object of his thinking. He endeavours no less than to *become* that which speculative reason and intuitive recognition have shown him to be the ultimate Real.

The various theories of the structure of the world have to be viewed from this particular angle. Thus the ontology suggested in the *Gītā* is not a sedulously erected *system* but a *map* for the yogin who sets out to explore the unknown territory that lies 'behind' the immediately apparent, visible, reality of concrete objects.

Sāṃkhya ontology as we encounter it in the *Gītā* and, in

varied cast, in all other Vedānta and Yoga schools, is fundamentally evolutionistic. It tries to explain the transition from the One to the Many, from the all-inclusive reality of the Ultimate Being to the multiplicity and fractionary reality of the phenomenal world.

According to the ontological conception of the *Gītā* the subject and the object of the spatio-temporal universe are both rooted, and intersect, in the Ultimate Reality. The transcendental subject is designated as *puruṣa*, the transcendental object as *prakṛti*. They are also respectively referred to in the *Gītā*[17] as the 'higher nature' (*parā-prakṛti*) and the 'lower nature' (*aparā-prakṛti*) of the Supreme Being. They are said to be the womb (*yoni*) of all contingent realities.[18]

The relation between Self (*puruṣa*) and non-Self (*prakṛti*) is rather recondite and has given occasion to various misinterpretations. It is quite wrong to interpret it as an 'eternal co-existence' which implies a clear-cut separation between both principles. R. C. Zaehner tried to avoid this fallacy by speaking of an '*ambiance* that is conditioned by neither space nor time nor change',[19] but this, too, is not entirely convincing. Terms like duality or non-duality are not really applicable to the reality that lies beyond the sway of space and time. *Puruṣa* and *prakṛti* cannot be made out to be distinct *entities*. They are the two *poles* of the One Being experiencing itself. To take an example from modern physics, their relation is similar to that which exists in the uniform phenomenon of light between particle and wave. They become separate, opposite entities only on the spatio-temporal level.

This *relative* dualism is in sharp contrast to the unqualified Dualism upheld by the Sāṃkhya system as first formulated by Īśvara Kṛṣṇa in his *Sāṃkhya-Kārikā*. Deviating from the epic Sāṃkhya, Īśvara Kṛṣṇa committed the devastating blunder of absolutising the empirical distinction between subject and object and postulating a pure subject confronting a *pure* object. This completely fictitious chasm between *puruṣa* and *prakṛti* gave rise to numerous other illogicalities and insurmountable metaphysical problems. God, in fact, is the knower and the known and also the process of knowing. 'God tastes Himself in all things.'[20]

Īśvara Kṛṣṇa also offered a number of arguments in support of the existence of Self and non-Self. In vindication of the existence of the Self he submitted the following points.

1. *Teleological argument:* The processes of Nature (*prakṛti*) are not mechanical and blind, but purposive. Nature serves the multiple transcendental Self-monads (*puruṣas*) as a basis for their world-experience as well as for their world-negation.
2. *Logical argument:* All evolutes of *prakṛti* are composed of the three types of primary quality, the *guṇas*; they logically presuppose the Self which is uncompound and beyond the *guṇas*.
3. *Ontological argument:* Empirical knowledge is impossible without a transcendental co-ordinating principle of pure consciousness.
4. *Ethical argument:* The experience of pleasure, pain, etc. has meaning only in so far as there is a conscious principle which experiences them, since Nature itself is unconscious matter.
5. *Mystical argument:* The desire for emancipation from the bonds of Nature, as apparent in some beings, presupposes the existence of that which is aspired to, namely the eternally free Self.

These overlapping arguments are, of course, no compelling proofs, or even satisfactory answers. Rather they appear to be desperate attempts at defending a system which on account of its autocratic logical approach, has stuck fast in fallacious abstractions and grave inconsistencies.

Kṛṣṇa shows no inclination to hunt for empirical proofs to establish his teaching. He deals not with abstractions and concepts, but with realities which he knows cannot succumb to compression into mind-bound systems. Consequently, the Self is for him not a concept gained through intellectual abstraction of the empirical fact of subjectivity, which stands in need of further proof, but the Self is its own proof. Kṛṣṇa here is faithful to the Vedānta tradition which has always maintained that the Self can never be made a datum of ordinary experience or reason. It is essentially intangible. It cannot be known in the common sense of the word, rather it reveals itself to itself within itself, in that 'state' which *yogins* and mystics regard as the ultimate consummation of spiritual life.

As opposed to the classical Sāṃkhya system which rigidly postulates a plurality of transcendental Selves, Kṛṣṇa teaches the Self to be a 'particle' (*aṃśa*) of the all-embracing Supreme Reality. He ignores the Sāṃkhya argument that if there was only one Self common to all contingent beings, then with the emancipation or Self-realisation of the first being all others would also be emancipated instantaneously, and he furthermore avoids the pure Monism of some upaniṣadic teachers. He wisely chooses to mediate between these two extreme alternative standpoints: The Self is one as well as many. The Selves of all beings are intersecting and fully participating in each other's selfhood.

> [He whose] self is yoked in Yoga [and who] everywhere beholds the same, sees the Self abiding in all beings and all beings in the Self. (VI.29)

From this it becomes clear that the Self is not merely a heterogeneous attachment to the personality complex of man. Instead it is the integrating centre of the psychosomatic 'field' of the human being. The *Upaniṣads* characterise the Self as 'observer' (*draṣṭṛ*) and 'witness' (*sākṣin*), and the *Gītā* follows this lead. However, as so many passages evince, it does not reduce the Self to a purely static principle totally isolated from the dynamic processes of the empirical being.

On the contrary, the Self, as a mode of the Ultimate Being which pervades everything, is the creative core, the regulating and connective force of the individual being. The *Kaṭha-Upaniṣad*, which closely reflects the spirit of the *Gītā*, employs the following simile to express the axial function of the Self in the human organism.

Know the Self (*ātman*) to be the master-of-the-chariot (*rathin*), the body as the chariot, the wisdom-faculty (*buddhi*) as the charioteer and the mind as the reins.
The senses, they say, are the horses, the sense-objects are their arena (*gocarān*).[21]

The Self is the life-giving nucleus of the human being. It is pure consciousness (*cit*) or, as Patañjali in his *Yoga-Sūtra* says, the power-of-consciousness (*cit-śakti*). This attribution touches on a highly controversial issue in both Eastern and Western philosophy, namely the crucial question whether consciousness exists apart from 'its' contents. Logical positivists, including the Buddhists, persistently deny the separate existence of consciousness. They arrive at this conclusion by subtracting from a conscious experience all its individual events till finally nothing is left at all, except nothing. A characteristic specimen of this type of logic-chopping argumentation is found in the *Milindapañha*. The following conversation is between Nāgasena and the Indo-Greek king Milinda or Menander:

Your majesty, if you came in a chariot, declare to me the chariot. Pray, your majesty, is the pole the chariot?—Nay, verily, bhante.—Is the axle the chariot?—Nay, verily, bhante.—Are the wheels the chariot?—Nay, verily, bhante.—Is the chariot-body the chariot?—Nay, verily, bhante...Is it, then, your majesty, something else besides pole, axle, wheels, chariot-body...—Nay, verily, bhante.—Your majesty, although I question you very closely, I fail to discover any chariot. Verily now, your majesty, the word chariot is a mere empty sound. What chariot is there here? Your majesty, you speak a falsehood, a lie: there is no chariot.[22]

Buddhism denies the existence of 'wholes'. This emphatic denial can best be understood as being a reaction against those trends in Indian philosophy which were misled into postulating that a whole is *more* than its parts—a logical error which is still perpetuated by certain thinkers. All that can be assumed is that a whole is *other* than its parts when these are logically isolated from the whole.

Consciousness, as the awareness of internal and external events, is an irrevocable empirical fact, and no amount of positivistic reductionism can shatter its existence as something which is *other* than its contents or presentations if they be considered separately. Consciousness and its contents form an organic whole. The empirical consciousness (*citta*), in its various structures, is eclipsed by, or contained in, the Primal Consciousness (*cit*). Being and Consciousness are identical. As Śaṅkara expressed it: *sattā-eva bodho bodha-eva ca sattā*, 'Being is Consciousness and Consciousness is Being'.[23] They are not aspects of the Supreme Reality, but they *are* essentially the Whole.

The *Gītā* does not challenge this fundamental dictum of all idealistic schools of philosophy. The Ultimate One is Being-Consciousness (*sac-cit*). The empirical processes of perception and knowledge are localised events within the infinity of this Being-Consciousness. On the temporal level the Being-Consciousness Whole splits itself into multiple subjects and objects. Yet these particularisations are not illusory as the Advaita-Vedānta and other monistic systems try to convey. They are modifications within the Whole. The individualised being (*jīvā*) is not the product of an omnipotent delusion (*māyā*). The Self or man, as the organic centre of his personality, is an essential constituent of the Primal Being-Consciousness. The Witness-Self innate in every human being is not merely the Supreme Being reflected in the temporal realm. It *is* in its own right. It is a vortex in the unfathomable ocean of Puruṣottama.

How is it that man is unaware of his essential oneness transcending space and time and that instead his knowledge is confined to the more pedestrian level of phenomenal realities?

Śaṅkara, the great adversary of Kṛṣṇa, explains this anomaly by introducing the concept of nescience (*avidyā*). It is nescience, he insists, which makes man see multiplicity where there is in truth only unity, and becoming where there is really only Being. Nescience, also called *māyā* or delusive power, is responsible for the appearance of the world phenomena. It is neither real nor unreal. It cannot be said to be real because it is annulled in the state of emancipation, when the Self 'awakens' to its eternal autonomy. Nor can it be called unreal, because experience shows it to exist. Śaṅkara fails to plot its cause. It is, he argues, really indefinable and inexplicable.

This exposition is highly provocative. Śaṅkara, a sworn monist, conjures up a power other than and second to the One Reality in order to explain away duality! That he leaves this power undefined does not alter the fact that it is extraneous to the Primal One. Indeed Rāmānuja, the founder of the *viśiṣṭa* school of Vedānta, finds no difficulty at all in demonstrating that the concept of *avidyā* is in crying conflict with Śaṅkara's unyielding Non-dualism.

Rāmānuja exposes this ineffable power of nescience as a mere concept which has no empirical base and which, moreover, is not even logically sound because Śaṅkara admits its indefinability. The teachers of the other non-advaitic schools exercise similarly scathing criticism on this doctrine.

Rāmānuja, whose teaching resembles that of the *Gītā* in many respects, may be held to be representative of Kṛṣṇa's own point of view on this matter. Characteristically, the term *avidyā* does not occur in the *Gītā* at all. Furthermore, the word *māyā*, which in Śaṅkara's terminology is a synonym of *avidyā*, has a decidedly different connotation in Kṛṣṇa's work, as can readily be seen from the following stanza.

For, this [whole universe] is my divine power (*māyā*), composed of the p rimary-constituents (*guṇa-mayī*), hard-to-transcend. (VII.14[a])

The term *māyā* obviously refers to Nature (*prakṛti*), one of the two fundamental modes of the Ultimate Being, the other being the Self or Selves. It is called 'divine' (*daivī*) because it is enshrined in the wholeness of Puruṣottama. The Great Being is the foundation of *māyā*. *Māyā* is not an immaterial entity which is neither real nor unreal and without any base. It is the creative activity of the Supreme Reality which 'twirls about' all contingent beings as if they were mounted on a machine (*Gītā* XVIII.61). It obscures man's Self-knowledge (VII.15), but it is not illusory itself. It is God's centripetal power which continuously re-creates the world and which can only be neutralised and transcended through the centrifugal pull existing within man's inmost centre, the Self. The *Kaṭha-Upaniṣad* gives an aphoristic mythological account of this centripetal tendency within the All-pervasive Being.

The Self-Existent (*svayam-bhū*) pierced the openings [i.e. the sense-organs] outward. Therefore one sees [what is] outward, not the Self within.[24]

But man is not doomed forever to 'take' God from without alone, as it were, through the phenomena or sense data. Kant was mistaken. He ignored the possibility of direct knowledge of the *noumenon*, the thing in itself. He believed, however, that through moral perfection it was possible to make contact with the noumenal reality. The Christian bias is evident in this attitude. Kant stopped short before mysticism, the avowal that man can awaken to the noumenon and have *unmediated* knowledge of it. In this he personifies the distinct divide that exists between Eastern and Western philosophy.

It is one of the fundamental convictions of Oriental thinkers that the Reality 'behind' or 'beyond' the phenomena is not entirely inaccessible. They fully agree with Kant that the Self or World-Ground or Being in its pure nakedness cannot be known or understood by the human mind nor grasped by the senses. An often cited passage of the *Bṛhadāraṇyaka-Upaniṣad* (IV.5.15) bears this out. There the celebrated sage Yājñavalkya instructs his wife about the nature of Self (*ātman*).

Verily, where there is duality (*dvaita*) there one sees one another, there one smells one another, there one tastes one another, there one speaks to one another, there one hears one another, there one thinks of one another, there one touches one another, there one knows one another. But where everything has become just the Self—then whereby and whom would one see? whereby and whom would one smell? whereby and whom taste? whereby and whom would one speak to? whereby and whom would one hear? whereby and of whom would one think? whereby and whom would one touch? whereby and whom would one know?—Whereby would one know him by whom one knows this all [i.e. the entire world of multiplicity]?—That Self is not this, not that (*neti-neti*). It is unseizable, for it cannot be seized; indestructible, for it cannot be destroyed; unattached, for it does not attach itself; [it is] unconfined, unafflicted, uninjured.—Lo, whereby would one know the knower (*vijñātṛ*)?

The Self cannot properly be described. When asked about the nature of the Self, the Zen master Tokuichi laconically replied: 'You are putting frost on top of the snow.'

The Self can never become an object of knowledge. It is its own object. It is self-illuminating. This unobstructed Self-Luminosity (*svayaṃ-prakāśa*) is 'realised' by way of the centrifugal tendency within the giant body of Puruṣottama. This centre-directed movement unifies the human consciousness and empowers it to transcend itself.

This is the sole objective of Yoga. It furnishes techniques which effectively block the externalising trend responsible for man's spatio-temporal consciousness. What Yoga demands is put succinctly by Plotinus, the father of Western speculative mysticism:

Shut your eyes and change to and wake another way of seeing, which everyone has but few use.[25]

III. THE EDIFICE OF THE WORLD

Man is a curious compound of the Infinite and the Finite, Being and Becoming. He is the Whole and 'whole part'. To show this, in the light of the wisdom-doctrine of Kṛṣṇa, was the task and purpose of the previous chapter. Having concentrated so far on the transcendental pole of man's being, the Self as a particle of the All-pervasive Reality, it is now necessary to scrutinise his material aspect, to look at man as an ensouled, living organism. To be able to do this satisfactorily, we have to scan first the imposing multidimensional kingdom of Nature, both in its visible and invisible or supra-sensuous aspect.

Just as the Self of man cannot be taken out of the context of the Whole, so his psychosomatic being cannot be treated in isolation from its natural environment. The Self is nothing without all the other Selves with which it shares fully and unreservedly the self-same Being. And on the empirical level, all entities partake of the same 'matter' and the laws governing it, and thus indirectly share each other's life. Everything depends on everything and is reflected in everything. Pythagoras is reported to have maintained that 'if there is one suffering soul in the universe, all other souls will be affected until that suffering soul is restored to health'. Exaggerated as this claim may seem, it contains a profound truth. This interdependence is one of the leading tenets of Eastern thought. It has its antecedent in the experience of total interrelatedness of archaic man. The Indian thinkers, as it were, have only 'retouched' and elaborated philosophically this basic experience.

There is a definite coordination in Nature which is so perfect that all man-made machines, however complex, shrink into insignificance. Nature is a gigantic living organism. In full cognisance of this fact, Rāmānuja called Nature the 'body' of the Supreme Being. Nature is a cosmos, not chaos. It is an interdependent field, a continuum of life forces. This is being more and more recognised particularly through the pioneering efforts of Systems Philosophy based on Cybernetic Research and Information Theory, as well as through the findings of ecologists and conservationists.

The latter have the thankless task of reminding their contemporaries that if the encroachments of human civilisation on Nature are not soon checked, this planet will before long be an unfriendly and uninhabitable place, at least for man.

As drastic and fatal as man's influence on his environment is for the survival of the higher organisms on this globe—from the point of view of the entire cosmos this is merely a minor event. This local unbalance will not affect the overall equilibrium of Nature. There are far more momentous disasters in the universe, like the explosion of supernovae or the collision of nebulae. Even these macrocosmic catastrophes cannot throw Nature out of balance. They are an essential part of her self-preservation. The universe, as modern Astronomy confirms, grows like the mythological Phoenix out of its own ashes. The disintegration and new formation of stars and nebulae are its pulse beats.

The complete coordination which the visible part of Nature exhibits points to her overarching unity in the invisible, transcendental realm. Kṛṣṇa is convinced: Nature in her perplexing multiplicity is God become finite and relative without losing as much as an iota of His absoluteness or wholeness. The process of unfoldment from the supra-sensuous unitary world-ground (*prakṛti-pradhāna*) to the multifarious structures on the empirical level, both inorganic and organic, has intrigued and mystified the Indian seers and thinkers many centuries before the intellectual Titans of Greece and Ionia, the path-finders of Western philosophising, began to be fascinated by this transition from the One to the Many.

There are several remarkable cosmogonic hymns in the *Ṛgveda*. They are still largely mythological accounts of the beginning of cosmic existence, but all of them illustrate the eager spirit of philosophical enquiry cultivated by the early Vedic colonists. The most acclaimed and certainly the most advanced of these early ponderings is the so-called hymn of creation (X.129).[26] This sublime piece of philosophical craftsmanship was, like the majority of the Vedic hymns, triggered off by a mystical experience. It is the prelude to all subsequent cosmogonic models, particularly the ontological system elaborated by the Sāṃkhya movement.

There was a considerable time lag between the germinal philosophical endeavours of the Vedic seer-bards and the cosmogonic theories as we encounter them in the *Mahābhārata* and the *Gītā*. In the period during which the compilation of the *Brāhmaṇas* took place, creative philosophising was at its lowest ebb. The priestly élite were preoccupied with codifying and consolidating ancient rituals and supplementing them with a suitable theology. Consequently they neglected to bring to fruition the promising seeds of philosophical speculation planted by their talented ancestors, the Vedic *ṛṣis*. Except for a single passage in the *Śatapatha-Brāhmaṇa*, a later work of this philosophically barren genre of literature, there is no reference to the question of the relationship between the One and the Many.

This was taken up again by the older *Upaniṣads*, and from then on it attracted the attention and challenged and spurred on the ingenuity of many great thinkers. Exemplary for the early upaniṣadic treatment of this important philosophical topic is the following extract from the *Chāndogya-Upaniṣad* (VI.2.1–4). The conversation is between the sage Āruṇi and his son and pupil Śvetaketu:

1. In the beginning, child, this entire [universe] was mere Being (*sad-eva*), one only, without a second. Of this [Single Being] some say: 'In the beginning this [universe] was Non-being (*asat*), one only, without a second; from that Non-being Being was born.'
2. He spoke [further]: How, child, could this be? How could Being

be born from Non-being? In the beginning, child, this [universe] was surely mere Being, one only, without a second.

3. This [Single Being] visualised[27]: 'May I become many, and procreate.'—It emitted heat (*tejas*). That heat visualised: 'May I become many and procreate.'—It emitted water. Therefore, whenever a person grieves [i.e. weeps] or perspires, water is produced from heat.
4. The water visualised: 'May I become many and procreate.'—It emitted food (*anna*). Therefore, wherever it rains abundant food is produced. Verily, food is produced from water.

This can be regarded as the earliest refutation of the well-known doctrine of creation *ex nihilo*. It epitomises the position of the entire Sāṃkhya movement which probably grew out of these incipient endeavours to explain the genesis of the manifold universe. The Sāṃkhya ontology is the first systematic and coherent account of the self-multiplication of the Ultimate Being. The beginnings of this important branch of Indian thought probably coincide with the awakening of the philosophical genius in Greece.

This ancient tradition was closely allied to the Yoga and the Vedānta movement. It is often pictured as the theoretical foundation of Yoga, but this is a rather crude simplification. Sāṃkhya, Yoga and Vedānta evolved out of the same intellectual soil. Their splitting into distinct rival systems was a slow process stretching over many generations of thinkers. In the centuries before the Christian era they were still intimately connected, although apparently independent schools had already been established. In the *Mahābhārata* as well as in the older *Purāṇas* and some of the *Upaniṣads* the three great traditions occur still in a flexible coalescence. The *Gītā* strikes the keynote of this whole fertile period of philosophising:

> Of yore I proclaimed a twofold way-of-life in this world, o Anagha [i.e. Arjuna]—the Yoga of wisdom for the *sāṃkhyas* and the Yoga of action for the *yogins*. (III.3)

The *sāṃkhyas* are, roughly speaking, introvertive contemplators whose main concern is the attainment of gnostic knowledge (*jñāna*) by cultivating detachment towards mundane things and leading a guileless and withdrawn life. The *yogins*, on the other hand, are extravertive mystics who seek the kingdom of God in an active life of pure deeds performed in the spirit of *inward* renunciation. Sāṃkhya and Yoga are essentially the same, also their ultimate goals are identical. As Kṛṣṇa states:

'Sāṃkhya and Yoga are different' say the simpletons, not the learned. Resorting properly to one [of these methods], one obtains the fruit of both.

That state which is obtained by the *sāṃkhyas* is also reached by the *yogins*. He who sees Sāṃkhya and Yoga as one, sees [rightly]. (V.4–5)

Although Kṛṣṇa sanctions the superiority of the path of action over contemplative life, he is not reluctant to make full use of the ontological 'map' provided by the Sāṃkhya phenomenologists. Plotinus, whose philosophical mysticism is an original 'recapitualation' of Vedānta metaphysics, posed this question:

Why did the One not remain Itself? Why did It emanate the multiplicity we find characterising being and that we strive to trace back to the One?[28]

The solution which he offered is in complete harmony with the answer given by Kṛṣṇa: the world of becoming is inherent in Being, 'the eternally perfect is eternally productive'. That this must not be taken as a mere logical conjecture but as an insight gained in a state of mystic illumination is already hinted at in the famous hymn of creation:

Seer-bards, searching in [their] heart with wisdom-thought (*manīṣā*), discovered the bond of Being in Non-being. (X.129.4[b])

On this crucial issue the Sāṃkhya philosophers propose a full-fledged theory of causation, the so-called doctrine of *sat-kārya*. This hypothesis, which is in disagreement with Materialism, early Buddhism and the Nyāya and Vaiśeṣika systems, purports that the effect pre-exists in its material cause. No effect is an entirely new creation. Rather it is the explicit manifestation of that which is implicitly present in its material cause. All material effects are a transformation (*pariṇāma*) of Matter (*prakṛti*). The world-ground, as the unmanifest and uncaused cause of all manifestation, contains every possible form of being in a state of latency. 'It is pure potentiality', says S. Radhakrishnan.[29]

The notion of *prakṛti* as the root-principle of all cosmic manifestations corresponds perfectly with the concept of *physis* in pre-Socratic philosophy. The primary meaning of both words is 'growth'. There is no single word in English which conveys the precise meaning of either term. Various renderings have been suggested, such as Material Nature, Primordial Matter and Ultimate Substance. Because of their marked materialistic tinge, they are all rather unsatisfactory. The term 'world-ground', used throughout this book, at least does not invite unfair misinterpretations of the essential character of this ultimate source of life. For, it would be absolutely inaccurate to suggest that *prakṛti*, or *physis*, is merely the common pool of 'dead' matter. On the contrary, it is a highly dynamic principle, the 'power' (*śakti*) of God.

Naturally, this sublime conception of a transcendental 'force field' which holds in latent form all the things that will ever come into existence, was naturally reached only gradually. Step by step mythology was replaced by bold philosophical enquiry. Thales of Miletus still saw the origin of all configurations of life in 'water'—thus repeating a cosmogonic model which seems to have been in vogue in ancient India.[30] And Anaximenes' doctrine of 'air' as the root-cause of everything has its exact counterpart in another favourite cosmogonic myth of India which derives every form of life from 'ether' (*ākāśa*).[31]

It was Anaximander who arrived at a philosophically more elaborate and consolidated doctrine. His concept of the 'limitless [world-ground]' shows a striking resemblance to the unfathomable One prior to being and non-being articulated for the first time in the hymn of creation. Anaximander had also given some thought to the actual process of world-creation, the flowing of the Many out of the One. At any rate, as far as one can judge from the fragments that are left of his work, his model of the stages of the cosmic genesis appears rather elementary in comparison with the highly complex hierarchical structure pieced together by the Sāṃkhya philosophers.

Prakṛti is the primordial matrix out of which all material *and* psychic phenomena evolve. Thus mind and matter are derivatives of the same principle. They differ in degree only. Mind precedes matter. Matter is solidified mind. This process of increasing differentiation of the One may be called cosmic evolution. The evolution of life on earth then appears as a particular instance, a local continuation of the macrocosmic process.

The emergence of the Many takes place in a recognisable order. As the divine matrix unrolls itself, it manifests the multidimensional structure of the universe. The hierarchic arrangement of the cosmos suggests comparison with a pyramid. The key-stone at the very top of the pyramid represents the unitary world-ground, its base is the realm of the particularised material objects, and the layers of brickwork in between symbolise the various categories of psychomental life, that is, the 'invisible' or 'spiritual' dimension of the universe. Creation is continuous. New forms of life do not emerge at random. The One Life pours itself out according to a definite pattern. Everything has its pre-ordained place. The different 'levels' of reality are the 'moulds' into which the original creative force flows as it were. Without this intrinsic order, creation would be totally unintelligible.

Prakṛti is a homogeneous, unparticularised universal 'field'. In Classical Sāṃkhya, *prakṛti* is defined as the state of equilibrium of the *guṇas*—a view which is tacitly assumed in the *Gītā*. What are these *guṇas*? They are ultimate *reals* inherent in absolutely every existing form. In Kṛṣṇa's own words:

> There is no entity (*sattva*) on earth, or again among the gods in Heaven who is free from these three [types of] primary-constituents (*guṇas*) born of the world-ground. (XVIII.40)

The *guṇas* constitute the entire manifest world. They are not only the irreducible ultimate foundation of the physical cosmos, but also the constituent units of all mental and psychic phenomena. One of the meanings of the word *guṇa* is 'strand' or 'rope'—and this alludes to their cohesive function; they 'hold' all manifest things together.

The *guṇas* are infinite in number, but belong to either of three types. There are *sattva-guṇas, rajo-guṇas* and *tamo-guṇas*. The mode of their manifestation in the diverse realms of the universe are delineated in numerous stanzas in the *Gītā*. Kṛṣṇa is understandably more concerned about the workings of the *guṇas* with respect to the inner world of man rather than with their cosmic effects. As a spiritual guide who sets out to lead man to greater self-understanding, he is naturally more of a psychologist than a physicist. This man-centred, existentialist approach is common to all schools of Indian thought. It is one of the main points of difference from Western philosophising which is object-directed.

A summary definition of the general nature of the triad of *guṇas* is given in the *Sāṃkhya-Kārikā*, the authoritative text-book of Classical Sāṃkhya:

The *guṇas* are of the nature of joy, joylessness and dejection and have the purpose of illuminating, activating and restricting. They overbear each other, are interdependent and productive and co-operative in their activities. *Sattva* is regarded as buoyant and illuminating. *Rajas* is stimulating and mobile. *Tamas* is inert and as it were concealing. The activity [of the *guṇas*] is purposive like a lamp [made up of various parts which together produce the single phenomenon of light]. (12–13)

Sattva means literally 'being-ness'. The primary-constituents of this type are responsible for the essential form—the 'idea' (in the Platonic sense)—of a thing which is to be realised during the course of its life. Of the three types of *guṇas*, *sattva* reflects most faithfully the condition of the One Being (*sat*). *Tamas*, on the other hand, is that power which obstructs the pure ascending tendency of *sattva*. It has a fixing, condensing, 'materialising' and externalising effect. And finally, *rajas* embodies the principle of activity which mediates between the 'idealistic lucidity' of *sattva* and the 'materialistic obscurity' of *tamas*.

This tripartite division is not a purely conceptual construct. It has an experiential basis. Yet it would be erroneous to allege that this analysis of the unitary ground of existence into three distinct modes defeats the notion of *prakṛti* as a uniform principle. For, the three kinds of *guṇas* are not radically separated from each other. They are merely phases or 'moments' of the same homogeneous energy field.

In the *Gītā* the *guṇas* are said to be produced from *prakṛti*. This has induced S. N. Dasgupta to think that they do not constitute the world-ground.[32] He seems to overlook the other occasions when the world-ground is referred to as *guṇa-maya*, that is 'composed of *guṇas*'. Dasgupta's somewhat rigid view is the direct result of his apparent failure to understand the exact meaning of the conception of God's 'higher' and 'lower' nature. He does not realise, it seems, that the 'higher nature' of the Supreme Being refers to 'what Teilhard de Chardin calls the "biosphere", the world of conscious beings',[33] in other words, the realm of the Self-monads or *puruṣas*. The *guṇas* and their interplay are restricted to the 'lower nature' of the all-encompassing Being.

The evolution of the Manifold is succeeded by its involution, its re-absorption into the unitary world-ground, only to be renewedly emitted after a period of mere potentiality. This periodic erection and decomposition of the universe is governed by the tension between the triune *guṇas*. When they reach a state of relative balance, the manifest world is drawn back into its unmanifest core. As soon as this equipoise is disturbed, creation sets in. In the *Mahābhārata* this alternating process within *prakṛti* is compared to a tortoise stretching out and withdrawing its limbs. Another favourite simile is that of a spider emitting and withdrawing its threads.[34]

What is the cause of this perpetual alternation between creation (*sarga*) and absorption (*pralaya*)? Kṛṣṇa remains silent on this point. The world-ground is rooted in the inscrutable

Will of the Divine Being. Creation and dissolution of the universe are part of its mystery. Kṛṣṇa is practical-minded. He cares for true gnosis only, not for lukewarm abstract theories.

In Classical Sāṃkhya the very same question proved a real pitfall. Unwilling to abandon his extreme dualistic position, its founder was forced to resort to the following bizarre notion: The disequilibrium of *prakṛti* which starts the cosmic evolution is caused by the mere proximity (*saṃnidhi*) of the as yet unliberated Self-monads.

Classical Sāṃkhya fails to explain how there can be any influence at all in view of the fact that it regards the world-ground and the many Selves as autonomous and mutually exclusive principles. Also, since there are always unemancipated Selves 'near' to the world-ground, manifestation should never cease to be. In this case *prakṛti* would never exist in its unmanifest state. In full recognition of the fact that there cannot be any real contact between the *puruṣas* and *prakṛti*, Classical Sāṃkhya offers the notion of an 'apparent contact' (*saṃyoga-ābhāsa*) as the scapegoat for the failure of its extreme dualism to account for evolution

The *Gītā* is free of such logical aberrations. Kṛṣṇa's survey of reality reminds one of the immensely suggestive yet unconventional brushwork of the later Japanese Zen painters.

The universe is not created all at once. Evolution takes place in definite stages.

> Earth, water, fire, wind, ether, mind and wisdom-faculty (*buddhi*) as well as the ego—these are the eight divisions of My [lower] nature.
> (VII.4)

This stanza of the *Gītā* mentions, in reverse order, the major categories of the evolutionary scheme recognised by all Sāṃkhya schools.

The first principle to emerge from the undifferentiated world-ground is *buddhi*. The primary meaning of this ambivalent term is 'that which is wake or conscious'. Cognate words are *buddha* ('the awakened one'), *budha* ('sage'), but also *budhna* ('core, depth'). The last-mentioned connotation of 'depth' is implicit in *buddhi*. For one can only awaken or bring to consciousness something which previously lay concealed 'at the very core'. Viewed from the ordinary waking consciousness—the final stage of evolution—*buddhi* is indeed hidden in the 'depth' of the inner world of man. There is no exact equivalent of this important word in the English language, simply because its underlying concept is missing. In the *Gītā*, *buddhi* is pre-eminently used in a psychological sense, and it appears to have both a general and a more specific meaning. I have specified these as 'wisdom-faculty' and 'wisdom' respectively, as called for in context.

Cosmically speaking, *buddhi* is akin to Rimbaud's 'l'intelligence universelle' and Huxley's 'Mind at Large'.[35] It, furthermore, corresponds with the 'mind' (*νοῦς*) in Plotinus' mystical philosophy and closely resembles the 'collective unconscious' formulated by C. G. Jung and his school. In Classical Yoga *buddhi* is also called 'pure beingness' (*sattā-mātra*). In Vedānta it is variously designated as 'golden germ' (*hiraṇya-garbha*) and 'lord' (*īśvara*).

Buddhi represent manifested but not yet individualised consciousness-being. In its cosmic aspect it is also called *mahat* or 'the vast'. It is the seat of all individualised psycho-mental structures as well as of the component elements of the physical reality. In other words, the subjective and the objective realities are still undifferentiated in this universal principle. The character of *buddhi* is determined by a preponderance of *sattva-guṇas*. It is the upper limit of Nature's scale. It leads a threshold existence, standing as it does between the unmanifest suprasensible world-ground and the manifest world in its full extension and diversity.

Evolution does not come to a stop with the constellation of *buddhi*. Spurred on by the primordial dynamism immanent in the world-ground, *buddhi*, in turn, gives rise to a subordinate level of existence, that of *ahaṃkāra*. This word literally means 'I-maker'. It is the principle of individuation. Like *buddhi*, it has a cosmic and a microcosmic or psychological aspect. It is responsible for the creation of all individual entities—men, stars or crystals.

Psychologically, *ahaṃkāra* appears as self-consciousness. S. Radhakrishnan remarks that *ahaṃkāra* 'is not what individualises the universal consciousness, since the individuality is already there according to the Sāṃkhya: It individualises the impressions that come from the outer world.'[36] This may be true of the ontology of Classical Sāṃkhya, but it cannot really be applied to those schools which, like the *Gītā*, display a pronounced integrative approach. Since man is thought of as an exact replica of the cosmos in its varied levels, the cosmic *buddhi* must necessarily be part of his inner organisation as well. Nevertheless, it would be misleading to interpret these individual *buddhis* as independent entities. *Buddhi* is essentially one and the same in every being. The fact that it is said to contain the individual fates of all beings does not contradict this assumption, since the lives of all individual entities are inextricably bound up with each other. This nexus is systematically formulated and ethically interpreted in the classical doctrine of *karma*.

Also *ahaṃkāra* as the principle of individuation must be a single entity, since it logically precedes all multiplicity. The essentially active nature of the 'I-maker' is determined by a prevalence of *rajo-guṇas*. *Ahaṃkāra* effects the crucial scission between subject and object. It divorces the unity of consciousness-being into multiple consciousnesses which front innumerable 'external' objects.

On the subjective side, *ahaṃkāra* produces the particularised mind (*manas*) together with the five cognitive and the five conative senses, and on the objective side it gives birth to the five subtle elements (*tanmātra*) and the corresponding five gross elements (*bhūta*). The subjective categories will be explained in the next chapter. We are, at the moment, only interested in the gradual differentiation of the one undifferentiate ground of existence in so far as it crystallises into the magnificent edifice of the macrocosm.

What are these subtle elements out of which the gross elements supposedly evolve? The authoritative textbooks are rather taciturn on this point. In the *Sāṃkhya-Kārikā* they are described as 'non-specific' (*aviśeṣa*) entities. Since they are prior to the senses and on a par with the mind, they cannot become objects of sensory perception. The only way by which they can be known is through the 'inner sense', the mind's vision.

They are the essences of the five sensory functions. B. N. Seal, who was the first to study the Sāṃkhya conception of Nature in any detail and relate it to modern physics and chemistry,[37] defined them as the energy potentials appertaining to the five sense faculties by which a sentient being receives information from the external world. S. N. Dasgupta elucidates:

The tanmātras possess something more than quantum of mass and energy; they possess physical characters, some of them penetrability, others powers of impact or pressure, others radiant heat, others again capability of viscous and cohesive attraction. In intimate relation with those physical characters they also possess the potentials of the energies represented by sound, touch, colour, taste, and smell; but, being subtle matter, they are devoid of the peculiar forms which these 'potentials' assume in particles of gross matter like the atoms and their aggregates.[38]

The *tanmātras* evolve progressively in this order: sound-potential, touch-potential, form-potential, flavour-potential and smell-potential. Without this synchronisation between the *tanmātras* and the sense-faculties sensory perception would be impossible.

The last stage in the complex course of evolution is reached with the formation of the five types of gross elements, the building blocks of the familiar physical universe. The division into five kinds of elements (*bhūta*) is, of course, not the result of a chemical analysis of the properties of matter. It is simply the outcome of reflection on physical matter as it affects the five senses. Hence Dasgupta's rendering of *bhūta* as 'atom' is arbitrary. The multifarious forms, organic and inorganic, which populate the visible universe are nothing more than varying aggregations of these five fundamental 'substances'.

This, in outline, is the ground-plan of the edifice of the universe as visualised by the Sāṃkhya phenomenologists. It varies only slightly in the different schools of the Sāṃkhya, Yoga and Vedānta movement, and it may be taken to represent the position of the *Gītā* fairly accurately.

At first sight this entire cosmogenesis seems grotesque. Indeed Western critics have not held back on scathing though indiscriminate criticism. Still, on closer examination one cannot help admitting that it is a remarkably consistent interpretation of reality.

Whether it is a completely faithful picture of it is a different matter. Bearing in mind the recent advances in Theoretic Physics, Holistic Biology and not least Parapsychology, it seems a fairly realistic, albeit skeletal delineation of reality. It would certainly be a challenging and profitable task to undertake a serious study of this ancient cosmological model in the light of modern science and philosophy.

In this context a word may be said about the methodology adopted by the Sāṃkhya thinkers. Sāṃkhya has been acclaimed to be the first rationalistic philosophy of the world.[39] This is an exaggerated and a misleading assertion. Sāṃkhya is not a specific philosophical system concocted in the brain of a single philosopher; rather it is the name given to a vast and widely ramified movement, the beginnings of which go back to a time when *logos* lay dormant in *mythos*.

The rationalistic system of Classical Sāṃkhya is merely the concluding phase of this great tradition, and most probably the deliverer of its final death-blow. The barrenness of this contrived rationalistic approach of Classical Sāṃkhya is by no means distinctive of the general attitude of the earlier schools. Hence for an examination and evaluation of this ancient tradition one has to pay attention to them. Historically speaking, Classical Sāṃkhya is parasitical. It lives off the vivifying creative genius of its predecessors without seeming to assimilate their basic attitude which is intuitive-descriptive rather than rational-analytical and holistic rather than dogmatic. K. B. Rao who investigated the historical development of Sāṃkhya arrived at the conclusion that

> the Sāṃkhya lost its ground not because it did not have the support of the traditions—either vedic or non-vedic—but because of its extreme rationalism and more than normal concession to popular realism.[40]

As is apparent from the introductory stanzas of Īśvara Kṛṣṇa's *Sāṃkhya-Kārikā*, Classical Sāṃkhya is based upon intellectual enquiry (*vijñāna*) and renunciation (*virāga*). The former was thought to equip the practitioner with a veritable picture of reality by the aid of which he could ascertain his true nature: the transcendental Self-monad (*puruṣa*) abiding in total isolation from the realm of Nature. Renunciation of all that which reason had exposed as non-self and inessential would then gradually lead up to the realisation of the Self.

Īśvara Kṛṣṇa evidently discards the most vital part of the Sāṃkhya-Yoga tradition, namely the practice of meditative absorption (*dhyāna*). It is clear that no amount of ratiocination, however sincere, if pursued at an intellectual level, could ever replace that creative inspiration and ennobling insight which comes through unconditional analysis of the depths of one's being, and the resultant attitude of inner openness towards the Supreme Being.

It is true that the one-sided attitude of Classical Sāṃkhya was anticipated and prepared by certain revolutionary schools already in the Epic period. A number of passages in the *Mahābhārata* refer to their atheistic systems and their exclusive reliance on 'book-knowledge' (*śāstra*) rather than on practical experimentation or personal verification (*pramāṇa*) as advocated by the *yogins*.[41] On the whole, however, the Sāṃkhya phenomenologists made full use of the highly developed introspective techniques of Yoga.

IV. MAN: THE JANUS-FACED BEING

The *Gītā*'s ultimate concern is man and his destiny. The *Gītā* shares with all other schools of thought the archaic conviction that man is the centre of creation. His place in the universe is unique, because only to him is it given to become fully conscious of the Creator indwelling in everything. He alone can realise that essential liberty which is the birth-right of all sentient beings: the undivided identity with the Supreme Being.

Modern scientists have impatiently objected against the notion that man holds the central position in the universe and derided it as one of early man's baseless phantasies. They point out that our globe is no more than an insignificant speck in the universe, and human life no more than a late side-branch of (animal) life on earth. True as this may be, it measures man against a purely materialistic yardstick. Scientists conveniently ignore the fact that man is a conscious—to be more precise, a self-conscious—organism. Any Anthropology which fails to acknowledge that consciousness is the most decisive determinant of man's being is as self-contradictory and futile as a Theology without God.

Self-consciousness is a unique force in the cosmos. In man it balances out, overrides and indeed turns to advantage the multiple shortcomings of the physical body inherited from some anthropoid form of animal life. To reduce it to the status of an accidental property of matter and to minimise its paramount importance for man, is giving a poor and completely indefensible account of reality. At best it furthers the cause of those who, out of mere ignorance, are busy preparing the annihilation of mankind: Conscious life turning against itself.

Blaise Pascal's intuition was correct: Man is a fragile but conscious reed. The scientists' objection against the idea of man's axial station in the universe misfires, for it fails to understand that by 'man' is not meant the human physical organism, but man as a mind-matter unity.

As a conscious being, man stands between the relative torpidity of animal life and the perpetual blissfulness of the angelic life of the *devas*. Put differently, he holds the central position between the furthest effluence of God, namely matter, and His nearest, the supra-sensuous realities existing in the 'spiritual' dimension of the universe.

From the point of view of consciousness, both the animal and the angelic life forms are static. The former are a manifestation of *tamas*, the power of inertia effective throughout the cosmos, and the latter are pure *sattva* creations. Human nature, on the other hand, is dynamic (*rajas*). Only man is able, though not without disciplined effort, to traverse in consciousness the various levels of existence. He can raise himself to the vertiginous heights of Universal Consciousness-Being or reduce his consciousness to the extent that the body assumes all the characteristics of inanimate matter. It is in this immense range of mobility along the vertical axis of existence, namely consciousness, that man's freedom lies. It is put into his hands to determine the direction of his dynamism—towards greater insentience or towards increasing awareness. This challenge of choice is with man all the time.

The question of personal freedom in the *Gītā* has been hotly debated by scholars. There are a few stanzas which seem to favour a deterministic viewpoint. According to some scholarly opinions on the *Gītā*, man is impotent to decide his own fate. But against this speaks the whole tenor of Kṛṣṇa's doctrine. The *Gītā* deals with the crucial ethical problem of right and wrong, and this in itself would be a farce if man had not the ability or power to choose between these two possibilities. Without this basic freedom, he would also be incapable of Self-realisation (*ātma-anubhava*)—the *summum bonum* of human life.

Man is subjected to different sets of laws. He cannot disobey the law of gravitation. If he is unsupported in mid-air he must fall to the ground like a stone. As a living organism he is subject to various biological laws which he cannot violate. These laws he shares with the animals but there is a law which he does not share with animals, a law which he can disobey if he so chooses. It is the law of *dharma* or right and wrong.[42]

Unlike Sartre who sees man convicted to be free and who denies any influence of the past on his decision-making, Kṛṣṇa is fully aware of the strong bonds that tie man to the past and restrict his freedom. Unhesitatingly he subscribes to the doctrine of *karman* or moral retribution, accepted by nearly all schools of Indian philosophy.

Karman is the moral law. It governs the psychic and mental life of man, just as the law of cause and effect regulates the physical universe. This law implies that whatever a person wills—be it expressed in thought, word or deed—goes to shape his future destiny. In the words of the illustrious sage Yājñavalkya:

> . . . Man (*puruṣa*) is of the nature of desire (*kāma*). As is his desire, so is his resolve (*kratu*). As is his resolve, so is his work (*karman*). As is his work, so is what he obtains.[43]

Man's life in the present is the sole outcome of his free will exercised in the past. He alone is the maker of his fate—greater freedom or bondage. His present condition is nothing but the crystallisation of his past volitional activity. In this sense, the past is always present in us and cannot be shaken off. A person's genetic disposition, his belonging to a certain family, social group, nation, culture and race, his educational possibilities and the opportunities which present themselves during his life—these are all determined by the law of *karman*. They curtail man's possibility of action, but they do not impair his free will and, above all, they do not exempt him from the full responsibility for all his volitional expressions.

The law of moral retribution is universally valid and incorruptible. Coleridge once wrote:

It may be more possible for heaven and earth to pass away than that a single act, a single thought should be loosened or lost from that living chain of causes with all the links of which the free will, our only absolute self, is coextensive and copresent. And this, perchance, is that dread book of judgment in the mysterious hieroglyphs of which every idle word is recorded.[44]

However, this law is not a blind mechanism. Rather it is an organic process which, like life itself, is teleological: It is the driving force behind the moral and spiritual maturation of man. The accusation that this doctrine is fatalistic and pessimistic is completely unfounded. For, although the past determines the present, the future always remains open. Life is self-creative, spontaneous, not inflexibly mechanical. Atomic Physics taught us the lesson that even in the realm of inorganic matter exists a certain degree of freedom: the causal law does not seem to apply on the level of the atom.

How does the moral law operate? The Indian thinkers are by no means unanimous on this point. Jainism, for example, speaks of *karman* 'substances' which enter the human being from 'outside' as it were and bind it to the cosmic wheel. In Buddhism, again, we have the curious situation that it denies the existence of an enduring subject (a 'doer'), but emphasises the continuity of its 'deed'. At this point one has to remember that in Indian terms the 'life' of a person is not consumed by the present life, that is from the moment of conception to the hour of death, but extends to all previous existences pertaining to the same Self-monad.

The link or continuity between these different embodiments is vouched for by the 'impressions' (*saṃskāras*) which volition leaves behind in the depths of consciousness. These impressions constellate, on the principle of similarity, groups or 'tendencies' (*vāsanās*). Together they form an overall pattern which stamps the specific character of the individual associated with this particular bundle of subconscious impressions. This, of course, presupposes the notion that consciousness survives death. And this has never been seriously questioned by the Indian sages. Here 'consciousness' naturally does not refer to the individual's capacity for 'object-awareness', for this disappears with the decomposition of the psychosomatic field (i.e. the body) at death.

One cannot determine what one is, but only what one will be. Clearly, this freedom of choice must be seen against the background of the particular forces that shape one's present type of existence. A life of seemingly insurmountable external oppression hardly favours self-determination. Nor do deep-rooted defects in one's character smooth the path for achieving that inner equilibrium imperative for exercising the faculty of true choice. Genuine self-understanding is a prerequisite for self-determination. It is to the extent that a man understands himself, that he is free. Only when he has become conscious of his conditioning, can he extricate himself from it. Man is *essentially* and unconditionally free. His self-determination lies in that he can either opt for or against this intrinsic freedom. In other words, he can deny or affirm his Selfhood, his true being which transcends space and time.

S. Radhakrishnan epitomises Kṛṣṇa's viewpoint when he suggests the following comparison:

> Life is like a game of bridge. We did not invent the game or design the cards. We did not frame the rules and we cannot control the dealing. The cards are dealt out to us, whether they be good or bad. To that extent, determinism rules. But we can play the game well or play it badly. A skilful player may have a poor hand and yet win the game. A bad player may have a good hand and yet make a mess of it. Our life is a mixture of necessity and freedom, chance and choice. By exercising our choice properly, we can control steadily all the elements and eliminate altogether the determinism of nature.[45]

Man is free to be free. This is Kṛṣṇa's triumphant message. This unshakable faith in man's essential liberty indirectly finds expression in the ancient Indian social order of which the modern Hindu society is but a poor reflection. Here man belongs to two great value-pyramids—the caste system (*varṇa*) and the order of life stages (*āśrama*). Both institutions are vertically orientated; that is to say, they are based on a hierarchical structuring of human values, with the realisation of Selfhood at the very top.

First and foremost, man is a member of one of the four castes (*catur-varṇa*). Originally, the caste system was no more than a practical application of the insight that people by nature differ in temperament and capacity. Later on it became associated with heredity. From then on it gradually deteriorated into an inflexible artificial system allowing only the formation of ever new sub-castes. In this degenerate form it provoked the criticism of indignant Western observers whose anger was kindled by the extreme separatism and snobbery displayed by the members of the highest caste, the *brāhmaṇas* (brahmins). Whatever significance the caste division may have in contemporary India, it played an all-important and *useful* role in the days of the great epics.

As the designation *varṇa* ('colour'), used for 'caste', indicates, the origin of this stratification of the Indian society is more likely to be found in the cultural and racial amalgamation that took place after the Āryan immigrants had settled in Northern India. In due course, 'colour of skin' assumed the new significance of 'colour of character'. It appears that the caste system was originally more an idealistic notion than a sociological actuality. The weakness of the caste system lies in that it is, after all, only an idealistic abstraction and, in real life, it tends to become rigid and bottlenecked.

Probably the earliest mention of the idea of caste is in the 'hymn of man' of the *Ṛgveda* (X.90). There the castes are described as arising from the cosmic body of the Primeval Being; the *brāhmaṇas* from the mouth, the warriors (*rājanyas*) from the arms, the artisans (*vaiśyas*) from the thighs and the serfs (*śūdras*) from the feet. These are the four castes. All those men who are excluded from this fourfold order are called *dasyus*, no matter whether they speak the language of the Āryan tribes or that of the *mlecchas* ('barbarians').[46]

Each caste has its allotted function and its own code. They are formulated in accordance with the intrinsic aptitude and talent of its members. Naturally much more is expected of the higher classes, and the responsibility of the *brāhmaṇas* for the lower castes weighs heaviest of all. The *brāhmaṇa* is the custodian of the spiritual heritage of his people. His duty is to act as a counsellor and teacher. He must exert himself to obtain spiritual insight and power so that he can guide the community, wisely and justly, and preserve and raise its moral strength. He should lead a simple life and not aspire after worldly possessions or even fame. Society will provide his means of subsistence.

The foremost task of the warrior (*kṣatriya*) is to protect his country and ensure the freedom of its people. He can enjoy all the power and pleasures of the well-to-do life of a soldier, but he must be prepared any time to lay down his life for the country.

The artisan's (*vaiśya*) business is the production and distribution of wealth. He is responsible for the material welfare of society. It is he who has to till the fields, protect the cattle and engage in trade.

Finally, the serfs (*śūdras*) are, as Kṛṣṇa says, those to whose very nature work is service (XVIII.44). They are the proletariat on whom, ultimately, depends the economic stability of a country.

In this connection the emphatic words of the Neo-Vedāntin Gerald Heard seem opportune:

Liberal, individualized Democracy is failing, failing politically against the Dictators, failing economically to solve its own internal stresses, from lack of organization. The disappointment over the limitations and failures of economic planning should show us that what we need before all such attempts is the laying of a foundation on which they may rest. Before economic planning we must have psychological planning.[47]

Such a psychological organisation, a concrete organic relationship between the various constituents of society, which is so lacking in modern democracies, is contained in the original model of the Indian caste system. Gerald Heard goes on to say:

Caste has no evil but only good if its two original and basic rules are observed: (1) that anyone who can qualify for the higher or highest ranks may and must be admitted (2) that the higher the rank the less has the individual any amusements or private possessions, while in the highest rank any office or direct power and influence must be ruled out.[48]

Gerald Heard then develops a grand utopian vision of a new society created by the 'neo-brahmin'—a new type of sage who has no rank or executive position in life, who is free of emotion and selfishness and who, above all, has sensory and mental powers beyond the ordinary. One may smile at this prophetic enthusiasm. But the urgency to find some kind of solution for the spreading disintegration of contemporary culture has not in the least diminished.

Along with their specific duties, all members of the three upper classes are enjoined to observe the tenfold 'common' moral code or *sādhāraṇa-dharma*, as given in the *Dharma-Śāstra* of Manu (VI.92). The ten virtues enumerated are: steadiness, forgiveness, self-control, abstention from unrighteous appropriation, purity, sense-control, wisdom, learning, truthfulness and abstention from anger. Clergymen (*brāhmaṇas*), warriors and artisans are collectively called 'twice-born'. This refers to the symbolic birth into the Vedic community through initiation. All twice-born men are entitled to the study of the Vedic scriptures. However, only the *brāhmaṇa* is allowed to teach. *Śūdras* or serfs are excluded from this privilege to learn the sacred lore. This is so at least in theory. There have been cases in which *śūdras* were raised to the state of clergymen by virtue of their impeccable character and innate wisdom. The story of the youth Satyakāma, who could not even name his father, is one such example.[49]

Although incomprehensible to the modern mind, this formal exclusion of the *śūdras* from the religious life has its philosophical justification in the theory of moral retribution (*karman*): A person is born a *brāhmaṇa* or a serf on the strength of his volition in a previous existence. Nevertheless, as we have seen, the doctrine of *karman* also implies that a serf need not be born a serf in a subsequent incarnation. Infallible observation of the moral code pertaining to his own caste will secure for him a birth as a twice-born, perhaps even as a *brāhmaṇa*. This sounds like empty promises designed to hold the proletariat in leading-strings. Perhaps in later times it became just that. After all, throughout the ages economic exploitation of the less favoured groups in society has been practised all over the world through the introduction of hypnotic religious ideals. Yet originally this esoteric teaching of *karman* and successive rebirths was free of any political ulterior motives. It was introduced into the Āryan community by ascetics who had 'seen', and it was certainly not the result of theoretical deliberations on the part of the ruling sacerdotal class. Religious and social life was still spontaneous and far removed from the rigidity and aridity of the later Hindu culture.

Finally, one has to remember that the fourfold division of the ancient Vedic society was not static. On the contrary it allowed for the possibility of an interchange between the four classes. Manu, the mythical law-giver, is quite explicit on this point:

> A serf becomes a *brāhmaṇa* and a *brāhmaṇa* a serf [by their conduct]. Know this [to apply also] to one born of a warrior or an artisan.[50]

That this liberal attitude was, even in the earlier days of Hindu culture, not always enacted in real life needs no explanation. At the time of the *Mahābhārata*, it was Yudhiṣṭhira who troubled his mind about this dissonance. And he missed no opportunity to reinforce Manu's broadminded convictions:

> Truthfulness, charity, fortitude, good conduct, kindness, austerity and sympathy—in whom these are seen he is called a *brāhmaṇa* . . .[51]

There is also the story of the fowler who obtained his present birth as a *śūdra* through the powerful curse of a sage whom he had accidentally wounded in the previous life. Although the sage could not reverse his curse, he offered this consolation to the fowler that his drop in social status would not mean the loss of his inner nobility and purity:

He who, though a *śūdra*, is always devoted to restraint, truthfulness and righteousness—him I consider a brahmin by virtue of his conduct: he is indeed a twice-born one.[52]

This liberal attitude towards caste is characteristic of the *Mahābhārata* as a whole. Kṛṣṇa, in the *Gītā*, teaches equality of all beings. Nobody is excluded from the search for the Supreme Reality, neither women nor serfs.[53] Whoever resorts to the Divine Being can be sure of relief from all suffering and is able to attain the supreme state of enlightenment.

Another typical instance is the story of Jājali, a proud clergyman who had to learn the bitter lesson that even a simple merchant who practises his profession with contentment can acquire spiritual powers and illumination. There is also the case of Droṇa, the leader of the army of the Kurus, who descended from a *brāhmaṇa* family. On the other hand, Bhīṣma the famous warrior held long discourses on philosophy, ethics and the high path to emancipation. There is also the outstanding example of the warrior Viśvamitra who became a famous and feared sage, and that of the popular king Janaka who instructed *brāhmaṇas* in the sacred lore.

And finally, was not Kṛṣṇa, the divine teacher himself, of *kṣatriya* origin?

The life of the twice-born members of the Hindu society unrolls in four great stages: that of the student (*brahmacārin*), the householder (*gṛhastha*), the forest-dweller (*vānaprastha*) and, last, the renunciant (*saṃnyāsin*). Ideally the first stage extended from birth up to the twenty-fourth year, the second stage up to the forty-eighth, the third up to the seventy-second year and the last stage from then on until death. Originally only the first two stages were known. By the time of the *Āraṇyakas*, the third stage had been added. In the *Mahābhārata* (XII.242.15) the four *āśramas* are compared to a ladder the upper part of which is attached to the Ultimate Reality.

The first stage serves as a preparation for the householder stage. The student or *brahmacārin* lives in the home of a reputable teacher whose task it is to instruct him in religious lore and the intricate art of rituals. For his efforts he expects the constant attention of the student. Pupilage is severe. All luxury is shunned. The pupil must beg his food and show absolute obedience to his teacher, whom he has to honour as the image of God. Particularly truthfulness and chastity are asked of him.

On completion of studentship, a man enters the householder stage. His foremost duty is now to marry and beget children. Sex, strictly forbidden during the period of pupilage, is carefully regulated. He must pursue an occupation which is in keeping with the laws of his caste. Guided by the wisdom accrued from the regular study of the Vedic texts, he is expected to work for the prosperity and welfare of his family and society in general. This *āśrama* is of the utmost importance to the whole community. In Manu's code (III.77) this is clearly emphasised:

> Just as all creatures live supported by air, so the other life-stages exist in dependence of the *gṛhastha*-stage.

A man may quit the householder stage and reture to the solitude of the forest, with or without his wife, when 'wrinkles begin to show, his hair greys and when he sees the sons of his sons'. Leading a simple ascetic life, he now concerns himself with sacrifices and the deeper study of the Vedic scriptures. Physical relationship with his wife is taboo.

Finally, renouncing even these religious pursuits and severing all connections with his family, his clan and society as a whole, he lives freely in the continuous presence of the Divine. His home is the whole world. His only care is for the Supreme Reality. Like the swan of mythology who could separate milk from water, he draws the nectar from the poison of the world.

Intimately connected with the concept of the four stages of life and the four castes is the notion of the four ideals of human life (*puruṣa-artha*), namely

artha	material welfare
kāma	cultural interests
dharma	normative behaviour
mokṣa	striving for emancipation as Self-realisation.

These ideals correspond to the various levels of human self-expression, that is, the physical, the emotional and the intellectual realm and, above and beyond these, the transcendent. These four goals are legitimate 'ends' and not inimical to spiritual life. *Dharma* runs like a thread through *artha* and *kāma* holding them together and aligning them with the *summum bonum* of life, the realisation of the Self.

The *Gītā* attempts an integration of these great goals and thus seeks to arrest the tendency of the epic age to overrate *mokṣa* and disregard the other three social values. However, the inclusion of the goals of *artha* and *kāma* does not mean that the *Gītā* gives the signal for blind hedonism. Man has to exercise control over his senses, whichever of the four goals he strives for and in whatever stage in life he may be.

The senses (*indriya*) are, as the *Kaṭha-Upaniṣad* contends, like unruly horses. If not kept in careful check by a stable mind, they easily bring disaster on a man. The sense-objects incessantly bombard the senses and tempt a person to establish a psycho-mental contact (*saṅga*) with them. He reacts to them with either attachment (*rāga*) or dislike (*dveṣa*). Unfulfilled desire (*kāma*) gives rise to disappointment and anger (*krodha*). This, in turn, leads to confusion (*moha*). Where confusion reigns, there is also a dispersion of mindfulness (*smṛti*). From this results the loss of the innate wisdom (*buddhi*) which practically completes the ruin of a person.

This evinces the superlative importance of sense-control—the mainstay of Yoga. The senses are continually fickle and draw the uncontrolled mind along their unsteady course.

[When] of the five senses of a person even a single sense is 'leaky' (*chidra*), then his wisdom (*prajñā*) flows away like water from the tip of a hose.

First the knower-of-Yoga must seize the mind as a fisherman [seizes] a slippery (*ku*) fish; and then [he must proceed likewise with] hearing, sight, taste and smell [as well as touch].

Tightening (*saṃyamya*) these [senses] in the mind, the ascetic should cause [them] to stand still; then, severing the mind from [its] desire-activity (*saṃkalpa*), he should hold it within himself (*ātmani*).

Restraining the five [senses] in the mind through knowledge (*jñāna*), the ascetic should cause [them] to stand still; then, when these together with the mind as the sixth [sense-organ] abide within himself and are tranquil and full at rest, the Absolute (*brahman*) shines forth.[54]

The functional interdependence of the five senses, the mind and the wisdom-faculty (*buddhi*) is illustrated in the following simile:

The body is said to be a town. The wisdom-faculty is considered the ruler. The mind abiding in the body is said to carry out the intentions of the wisdom-faculty.

The senses are the townsmen. Their principal duty (*kṛti*) is to fulfil the intentions of that ruler.[55]

There is a natural disparity among people. Everyone pursues his own interests. Without some form of regulation this would soon end in a general clash of ideas and life styles. To create a common law which mediates between the personal and the larger social interests is the foremost obligation of the sovereign! His wisdom and steadfastness will exercise a decisive influence on the attitudes of his people. However, he must be able to rely completely on his Minister who reinforces his orders and keeps him informed about the opinion of his subjects. The Minister fails in his office when he shows a bias towards the one or the other pressure group. It is self-evident that integration depends as much on the sovereign as it does on the Minister and the public. That is to say, sense-control is impossible without the curbing of the mind, and the mind remains fickle as long as the steady light of guidance from the wisdom-faculty is lacking. So, ultimately, it is *buddhi* which is the source of all tranquillity and harmony in a person.

Only *buddhi* can vanquish and transform the dark aspect or, as Nietzsche called it, the Dionysian nature of man. It is that principle by which the 'self is raised by the Self'. It is not simply 'reason' or 'intellect', but *inspired* reason; not aggressive thought, but receptive intuition; not the organ of analysis, but of synthetic vision. Like all other psychological terms used in Sāṃkhya and Yoga, *buddhi* connotes a psychic *faculty* and its corresponding *function*. In other words, it is not only 'illumination' or 'higher knowledge', as in Vedānta, but at the same time also the 'seat-of-wisdom', or 'organ-of-intuition'. In *buddhi* the pattern of the Whole is reflected. Its essence is 'will' (*vyavasāya*). It knows activity (*pravṛtti*) and cessation (*nivṛtti*), what should be done (*kārya*) and what should not be done (*akārya*), fear and fearlessness, bondage and liberation, the norm (*dharma*) and what is inimical to the norm (*adharma*).[56]

By way of contrast, the lower mind (*manas*) has no illuminating or creative power. It acts merely as the rallying-point of the senses. Whereas *buddhi* gives birth to unifying knowledge, *manas* busies itself with parts; it is mechanical and analytic. Yet although the lower mind often operates in disharmony with, if not against, the wisdom-faculty, this must not be taken to signify an acute breach between these two components of man's psycho-mental organism. The activities of the analytic mind, the *sensorium commune*, are always carried on against the background of *buddhi*.

As the centralising and integrating psychic principle, *buddhi* is the primary instrument of Yoga.

Restraining the agitated senses, which fly out in all directions, through the wisdom-faculty with [proper] exertion,—like a father [controls] his own sons—[this] one-pointedness of mind and senses is the most excellent [form of] asceticism.[57]

Unless the serene luminosity of *buddhi* penetrates into all parts of his mind and psyche, a man is a slave to the conditioning resulting from previous existences and from the impact of social and other environmental forces in the present life. In that case self-determination is as unreal as any day-dream, and action springs from passion, greed, utilitarian charity, selfish love, hidebound considerations, or simply sheer ignorance.

On the other hand, when *buddhi* assumes dominion over the personality and pours its light into even the darkest recesses of man's inner world, there will be a total upliftment of his being. This will manifest in an uninterrupted sense of increasing Self-approximation and inner harmony which will spread all around him and visibly affect his environment. The world becomes as if transparent to him, and everywhere he begins to behold the presence of the Supreme Being.

Reaching the apex of the ascending spiral of spiritual life, he drops even the last veil of nescience and breaks through to the inmost core of his being, the omnipresent Self (*puruṣa*). He awakens to his essential oneness with God, as a cell might awaken to its cellhood within the structure of an all-comprising organism. This is the beginning of a creative relationship, essentially incomprehensible but unfailing, between the Whole and the part which has become whole.

V. YOGA—PATH OF TRANSFORMATION

The *Gītā*'s message calls on man's Apollonian nature. He is asked to re-orientate his mental aspirations and transform his purely instinctual-sensuous existence into a wholesome life guided by spiritual forces. Blind following of the impulses of one's lower, Dionysian nature inevitably leads to disaster. There are other aspects of his being which await expression. Man has to order and harmonise his life, modelling it on the cosmic order (*ṛta* = *dharma*). Ordinarily, he is swayed by the three primary-constituents, the *guṇas*. He wavers between purity-calmness, passion-fickleness and inertia-ignorance—the respective manifestations of *sattva*, *rajas* and *tamas*. All his suffering, anxiety and unhappiness result from this continuous vacillation within himself.

Man's greatest failure and misfortune is his attachment to transient things. He clings to sensual things and the ephemeral delight they bring, as if his life depended on them; and he reacts wildly against anything which causes discomfort or inconvenience. Seeking pleasure and avoiding pain, he drifts along the path delineated by the pair of opposites (*dvandva*), like a boat without helm, all the while thinking that he has full control over the rudders of his life-ship.

Only when he realises that this is a self-delusion and when he assumes real control over himself by yoking mind and senses, does this erratic inner activity change and gradually give way to a more wholesome balanced state. The first step towards bringing order into the chaos of his mind is by assuming an attitude of creative openness towards his higher nature, the innate light of wisdom. Only thus can he break the deadlock to which his spiritual impoverishment and arbitrary attitudes have driven him.

For every individual there comes an hour sometime or other, for nature is not in a hurry, when everything that he can do for himself fails, when he sinks into the gulf of utter blackness, an hour when he would give all that he has for one gleam of light, for one sign of the Divine . . . The invisible impulse to seek God produces the agony that inspires heroic idealism and human fulfilment. The image of God in us expresses itself in the infinite capacity for self-transcendence.[58]

There is no prospect of ever escaping the vicious circle of man's self-made conditioning and the unhappiness resulting from it, unless *buddhi* is given room within his psyche. The higher wisdom or dispassionate enlightened understanding which *buddhi* pours freely into his mind is able to melt away even the most solid mental blocks and rocklike emotional attachments. Given a chance, the wisdom-faculty (*buddhi*) assumes mastery over the inner world and step by step brings order and light into the chaos. As a man becomes more even-tempered, calm and serene through the influence of *buddhi*, so he can tap the resources of the wisdom-faculty more and more consciously. There comes a point when he becomes fully aware of the 'essential form' of his particular life. For, the wisdom-faculty holds what Meister Eckehart called the *bild* or central 'image' which constantly seeks realisation in one's life.

Just as the chromosomes are responsible for the shape and the physical peculiarities of the mature human body, so the 'image' in *buddhi* determines the character of the inner evolution of a person, that is, his spiritual growth, as a being who is both immanent and transcendent. This is what is meant by the teleology of Nature (*prakṛti*). Everything strives to realise its own innate 'idea'. This process of self-realisation extends to all forms of life, and it can even be discerned in the inorganic realm, as for example in the surprisingly regular formation of crystals.

Every living being develops and matures according to an immanent pattern or law. One can, in other words, only become what one, in essence, already is. As opposed to crystals, man's path of self-realisation is studded with stumbling blocks. They arise from his conscious ego which overshadows the innate pattern, often to the extent that it becomes so obscured as to deprive his life of all deeper significance. The pressure of the unfulfilled innate 'idea' of what he is supposed to be and the antagonistic ideals which his conscious ego sets up, cause his life to be more of a serpentine path with innumerable *cul-de-sacs* than a straight line.

He must realise that he will never reach the top of the mountain, unless he becomes conscious that the circuitous route of his life is the result of his denial of the essential 'idea' within him, and that therefore he is in constant enmity with himself. Transgressing the inner law, he alone is responsible for the labyrinth of his destiny. It is unlikely that the unsettled course of his life will change, until he consciously struggles to dig out his essential being from underneath the massive structure of false concepts and values. This is the field of Yoga—the path of conscious self-realisation.

Yoga is a frontal attack on the fixed patterns of thinking and feeling acquired in the course of one's life. It aims at emancipating the 'innate idea' hitherto buried in the depths of one's psyche by scraping off layer after layer of false identifications and other worthless psychomental deposits. Yoga means a systematic pursuit of self-realisation leading to the recovery of the Self, man's inmost essence. It is in this conception of the Self as a supra-personal transcendental entity that Yoga departs from the individuation process of modern psychotherapy. In the nomenclature of the latter, 'self' appears to be an almost exact equivalent of *buddhi*, although C. G. Jung wisely left the boundaries of this 'self' undefined, wherefore these two concepts cannot be said to fully coincide.

Yoga has a long history. Already in the *Gītā* which, as we have seen, belongs to the pre-Christian era, it is called 'archaic' (*purātana*). Its earliest beginnings reach back to the time of the

Ṛgveda and, some scholars think, of the Indus civilisation which flourished in the third millennium B.C. Originally it probably has grown out of shamanistic practices which were customary in early man. I have shown elsewhere that the birth of Yoga has to be connected with the peculiar mental and perceptual ability of our ancestors, whose picture of the world we just begin to understand with the aid of the revolutionary findings of Parapsychology.[59]

It is not possible here to follow up the earliest stages in the development of Yoga, since little research has been done on this subject and a synoptic delineation would merely throw up many questions which could not be answered in this context. It must suffice to point out the continuity in the evolution of Yoga. The Yoga expounded by Kṛṣṇa is, as the divine teacher himself affirms, a restoration of older traditions which had been forgotten in the course of time. There is indeed little in the *Gītā* which cannot, albeit in germinal form, be detected in the one or the other hymn of the *Ṛg-* and *Atharvaveda*. Kṛṣṇa's outstanding achievement lies in that he injected new vitality into older teachings and elaborated them in a coherent manner.

The *Gītā* is held to be the textbook of theistic Yoga *par excellence*. According to the colophons, each chapter propounds a different type of Yoga. The following tabulation gives a fair idea of the degree of priority which Yoga enjoys in the *Gītā*; and indirectly also of the extreme plasticity of this term.

chapter I	*arjuna-viṣada-yoga*—'Yoga of the dejection of Arjuna'
II	*sāṃkhya-yoga*—'Yoga of contemplation'
III	*karma-yoga*—'Yoga of action'
IV	*jñāna-yoga*—'Yoga of wisdom'
V	*karma-saṃnyāsa-yoga*—'Yoga of renunciation in action'
VI	*dhyāna-yoga*—'Yoga of meditative-absorption'

VII *jñāna-vijñāna-yoga*—'Yoga of wisdom [and] [wordly] knowledge'

VIII *akṣara-brahma-yoga*—'Yoga of the Imperishable Absolute'

IX *rāja-vidyā-rāja-guhya-yoga*—'Yoga of the royal science [of inner wisdom] [and] the royal mystery [of the Supreme Being]'

X *vibhūti-yoga*—'Yoga of the power-manifestations [of God]'

XI *viśva-rūpa-darśana-yoga*—'Yoga of the vision of the all-form [of God]'

XII *bhakti-yoga*—'Yoga of love'

XIII *kṣetra-kṣetrajña-vibhāga-yoga*—'Yoga of the distinction between the field [and] the knower-of-the-field'

XIV *guṇa-traya-vibhāga-yoga*—'Yoga of the distinction between the three primary-constituents'

XV *puruṣottama-yoga*—'Yoga of the Supreme Being'

XVI *daiva-āsura-saṃpad-vibhāga-yoga*—'Yoga of the distinction between divine [and] daemonic [principles]'

XVII *śraddhā-traya-vibhāga-yoga*—'Yoga of the distinction between the three [kinds of] faith'

XVIII *mokṣa-saṃnyāsa-yoga*—'Yoga of emancipation [through] renunciation'

These are, of course, not distinct paths, but merely phases or aspects of the unitary life of the *yogin*. Each title is supposed to represent the kernel of the particular theme of a chapter in the *Gītā*.

The term *yoga* counts among the more ambiguous words of the Sanskrit language. It is used in the sense of 'team, vehicle, application, means, union, connection, profit, zeal', and has a great many more connotations. It is derived from the root √*yuj* 'to yoke'. In the *Gītā*, the word is used in a specific sense, yet without losing much of its ambiguity. There its principal meaning is undoubtedly 'yoking' or 'harnessing' or what R. C. Zaehner skilfully called 'integration'. It is the 'joining together' of our fragmented self, the yoking of our mind which seems ever ready to 'fly out' through the senses, continuously hankering after sense-pleasures.

One can clearly distinguish between several nuances of the word *yoga* as used by Kṛṣṇa. It means:

(i) *practical discipline* in contrast with the contemplative approach of the Sāṃkhya followers (see II.39);
(ii) the practice of *yoking* the self by the power of the wisdom-faculty (see II.48, etc.)
(iii) by definition, 'sameness' (*samatva*) (see II.48);
(iv) 'skill in [performing] actions' (see II.50);
(v) 'disunion of the union with suffering' (see VI.23).

As can readily be seen from this list, *yoga* stands for both the *process* and the *goal* of self-integration or harmonisation. It must be emphasised that these definitions are by no means mutually exclusive. It would be far more correct to regard them as focal points having all the other shades of meaning in the back.

Traditionally, the first six chapters of the *Gītā* are believed to expound *karmayoga*, the next six *bhaktiyoga*, and the last six *jñānayoga*. But this scheme is unconvincing. However, there are three central themes in the teaching of Kṛṣṇa. They are wisdom (*jñāna*) based on the realisation of non-duality, action (*karman*) performed in the spirit of unselfishness, and devotion or love (*bhakti*) towards the Divine Being. These correspond to the intellectual, volitional and emotional aspects of the human mind. In keeping with modern psychology, Kṛṣṇa does not believe that there is or should be a watertight division between them.

On the contrary, he stresses their homogeneity. Man is not exclusively a thinker or an agent or a feeling entity. He combines within himself all three faculties, though he may have developed the one more than the other. Accordingly, Kṛṣṇa's Yoga is a unique synthesis of action, thought and emotion or, by way of analogy, body, mind and psyche. His integral doctrine cannot be classified as either *jñānayoga*, *karmayoga* or *bhaktiyoga*. It incorporates and gives due weight to the essential features of all three avenues to emancipation and therefore comes nearest to the ideal of a holistic or *pūrṇayoga*.

Kṛṣṇa's attitude is liberal and quite unlike the dogmatic insistence of the Buddha that there is only one path to emancipation—namely the Noble Eightfold Path taught by himself. Kṛṣṇa endeavours to achieve a real synthesis without trying to simplify or unify the multifariousness of life. Therefore all attempts to label his integral doctrine or identify it exclusively with the one or the other type of Yoga is bound to fail.

Ignoring Kṛṣṇa's own testimony, Śaṅkara shows misplaced perseverance in his struggle to prove the supremacy of *jñānayoga* in the *Gītā*. According to him, *karmayoga* is merely a preparatory stage for those who have not yet ascended to the full heights of the wisdom of non-duality. His chief antagonist, Rāmānuja, on the other hand, identifies Kṛṣṇa's gospel with *bhaktiyoga*. Modern interpreters, again, who have before their eyes the disconsolate effects of a purely ascetic culture, tend to stress *karmayoga*. In response to this K. N. Upadhyaya has compiled a useful concordance which shows the amazing interdependence of the various 'paths', thus clarifying once and for all the integral character of Kṛṣṇa's Yoga.[60]

Anticipating C. G. Jung's working hypothesis of the two basic characterological types, the introvert and the extrovert, Kṛṣṇa says:

Of yore I proclaimed a twofold way-of-life in this world, o Anagha —*jñānayoga* for the [followers of] Sāṃkhya and *karmayoga* for the *yogins*. (III.3)

Renunciation and *karmayoga*—both lead to the *summum bonum*. But of the two, *karmayoga* is more excellent than [mere] renunciation. (V.2)

The adherents of the Sāṃkhya are here said to follow the Yoga of wisdom (*jñānayoga*), whereas the Yoga of action (*karmayoga*) is held to be characteristic of the *yogins*. The former is the path of contemplative men who renounce the world in favour of the transcendental Self. The latter is the path of the active-minded. Kṛṣṇa declares that both paths ultimately lead to the same goal, but renunciation *in* action is superior to renunciation *of* action. Why?

The answer is implied in Kṛṣṇa's concept of God as the all-inclusive Reality outside and beyond which there is naught. The world presented to our senses is a real component of the infinite body of God. Renunciation of all mundane activity is, to be sure, a radical antidote to man's precarious situation, but it is based on a fundamental misconception of the nature of the world. The followers of this path are unaware of the irrevocable fact that life means activity and that therefore no living being can sever itself totally from all action.

For, not even for a moment can anyone ever remain without performing action. Every [being] is unwittingly made to act by the primary-constituents (*guṇas*) born of the world-ground. (III.5)

The divine teacher sets himself as a model:

For Me, o son-of-Pṛthā, there is nothing to be done in the three worlds, nothing ungained to be gained—and yet I engage in action.

For, if I were not untiringly ever to abide in action, people would, o son-of Pṛthā, follow everywhere My 'track'.

If I were not to perform actions, these worlds would perish, and I would be the author of chaos (*saṃkara*), destroying all these creatures. (III.22–24)

The primary-constituents of the world-ground drive on the powerful machinery of the universe, and there is nothing which is exempt from their ceaseless activity. Contingent existence is a continuous process of becoming. In this respect Kṛṣṇa is in unanimous agreement with the Buddha and modern Physics. Not even the sage can call a stop to this incessant activity which sustains and is the very structure of his body and mind. Death, too, is a process and hence no escape route. Only God, in his transcendental aspect, is beyond the rule of the *guṇas*. Nevertheless, this does not imply that He is a static entity. In the *Gītā*, God is exalted as an infinitely dynamic reality, unlimited life. The difference between His inscrutable creativity and the activity of the *guṇas* lies in that the latter appertain to the spatio-temporal world, whereas there are no limitations to the Supreme Being.

Kṛṣṇa draws our attention to the fact that . . .

> even the man-of-wisdom behaves in accordance with his innate nature. [All] beings follow nature. What will repression (*nigraha*) accomplish? (III.33)

Wisdom does not abolish Nature's activity. It is of a totally different order. A side-glance at the peculiarities, the personal 'hue' of some great sages will confirm Kṛṣṇa's point of view: Although the Buddha regarded man as a mere fiction, he nevertheless wandered through Northern India preaching his doctrine for the enlightenment of his contemporaries; Śaṅkara, similarly, saw in the phenomenal world only an illusory appearance and yet devoted all his life to writing and teaching; in more recent times, the South Indian saint Ramana Maharshi may serve as an example: totally devoted to the realisation of the non-dual Reality, he still continued to write moving hymns and humorous songs for the inspiration and edification of his followers:

Kṛṣṇa rebukes the idea that action (*karman*) and wisdom (*jñāna*) are incompatible.

> 'Sāṃkhya and Yoga are different' say the simpletons, not the learned. Resorting properly to one [method], one obtains the fruit of both.
>
> That state which is obtained by the followers-of-Sāṃkhya, is also reached by the followers-of-Yoga. He who sees Sāṃkhya and Yoga as one, sees [rightly]. (V.4–5)

The split between the Creator and His creation is artificial, a fatal error of the intellect. Life need not be forsaken for the

Supreme Life which is omnipresent and therefore embraces conditioned existence. As the late Mahāyāna Buddhists exclaimed: *saṃsāra* is *nirvāṇa*—the wheel of becoming is no other than the absolute stillness of Being.

For Kṛṣṇa these metaphysical reflections suffice to derive an activistic ethics from them, the ideal of *karmayoga*. Kṛṣṇa thinks that a purely contemplative life is beset with a great many obstacles. He points out that it is all too easy to betray oneself by remaining outwardly inactive and withdrawn from the world, yet cherish inwardly unknown to oneself a host of desires. An active life in the world is according to him the best touchstone of one's real inner achievements. He does not condemn the attitude of genuine renunciation in principle, and he certainly does not wish to standardise human behaviour and turn everybody into a *karmayogin*. His emphasis on life in the world springs from the deep insight that few are really ready to lead a withdrawn, self-sufficient life with benefit, that is, which results in self-conquest and not self-deception.

This must not be misconstrued as a summons for complete immersion into social life. Over-activity is as out of place as inactivity. The *Gītā* favours neither self-indulgent asceticism nor hedonism. It censures both the almost hypochondriac passivity of the 'drop outs' and the restless competitive spirit of the overwrought business tycoon. Instead it offers a wholesome middle path: an active life in accordance with the rules related to one's particular stage in life, while at the same time engaging in the cultivation of inner wisdom. This is formulated in the doctrine of renunciation *in* action.

> In action alone is your rightful-interest, never in [its] fruits. Let not your motive be the fruit of action, nor let your attachment be to inaction (*akarman*). (II.47)

Every local activity effects a change in the entire structure of the space-time continuum. Any action which we perform indirectly affects the whole organism of the manifest universe. Because of this, Śaṅkara and his followers believed that no action could ever be conducive to the emancipation from the fetters of causality.

> Action is [only] for the purification of the mind, nor for the perception of Reality (*vastu*). The realisation of Reality is [brought about] by [true] discernment (*vicāra*), not in the least by millions of acts.[61]

> Not by Yoga, or Sāṃkhya, or [ritual] acts, or learning, but by the recognition (*bodha*) of one's identity with the Absolute is emancipation possible, and by no other [means].[62]

Śaṅkara is uncompromising. As long as there is in our psyche even the slightest tendency to act and enjoy, there is not the faintest prospect of emancipation. All work leads only deeper into the thicket of conditioned existence. Action binds and crucifies man on the cosmic wheel. As the author of acts, we are morally responsible for their repercussions, whether they be apparent or unseen. The chain reaction which we start off with each single act always abides with us and shapes our destiny. Like a caterpillar we spin ourselves more and more into a tight cocoon.

Only knowledge of the Self can emancipate us from the web of ignorance. This 'knowledge', however, is not a function of the intellect. Otherwise it would still be within the domain of Nature's activity. It is not knowledge in the ordinary sense, for it has no object. Self-realisation is rather the Self (*ātman*) revealing itself to itself. He who knows the Absolute, *becomes* the Absolute. This instant self-revelation is independent of our will. No means lead to it. Acts, provided they are of a wholesome (*puṇya*) quality, are merely auxiliary (*sahakārin*) to the attainment of emancipation, in as much as a person who no longer lives for transient joys and is not swept by passion or hatred, is ready for the great transforming experience.

Kṛṣṇa accepts in principle Śaṅkara's contention that only gnosis or *jñāna* reveals the Self. He differs from him only in that he fails to perceive an unbridgable chasm between gnosis and action. Whilst it is true that the Self shines forth only by reason of the liberating wisdom (which is not distinct from the Self itself), it could not do so unless the ground was prepared by yogic and other cathartic processes. The light of the Self never ceases to shine. That we do not perceive it, is due solely to the dust which has accumulated in the course of many existences on our mental mirror. Śaṅkara tends to play down the instrumental role which purificatory means play for the attainment of Self-realisation. Kṛṣṇa duly emphasises the value of both gnosis and action.

Since there can never be an end to activity, because activity is the very essence of the world, Śaṅkara and, even more so, the Buddha demand complete abstention from all action, that is, the progressive creation of an internal *and* external void. Renunciation is thus primarily *detachment*.

With Kṛṣṇa, renunciation assumes an entirely new significance. It is not cutting oneself off from the world, but disinterestedness as an *inner* attitude of dispassionate same-mindedness. In other words, he brings the mind as the main spring of all external deeds into full focus. We have to shake off not the actions as such, but their underlying egocentric motive forces. Stringent control of the mind prevents sin to enter our deeds. It is the thoughts which defile us, not their physical expression in the form of acts. Kṛṣṇa admonishes his confused disciple:

Holding pleasure and pain, profit and loss, victory and defeat as alike, gird yourself for the battle. Thus you will not heap sin [on yourself]. (II.38)

Steadfast in Yoga perform actions abandoning attachment, o Dhanaṃjaya, and remaining the same in success and failure.—Yoga is called equability (*samatva*). (II.48)

The *buddhi*-yoked leaves behind here [in this world] both good and evil. Hence yoke yourself to Yoga. Yoga is skill in [performing] action. (II.50)

He who restrains his organs-of-action, but sits remembering in his mind the objects-of-sense, is called a hypocrite [with] bewildered self.

But more excellent is he, o Arjuna, who controls with his mind the organs-[of-action] and, with the organs-of-sense embarks unattached on *karmayoga*. (III.6–7)

This world is action-bound, save when this action is intended as sacrifice.
With that purpose [in mind], o son-of-Kuntī, engage in action devoid of attachment. (III.9)

Hence always perform, unattached, the right (*kārya*) deed, for the man [who] performs action without attachment obtains the Supreme [Being]. (III.19)

These quotations from the *Gītā* make it crystal clear that the life of the recluse must be the exception rather than the rule. Man ought not to negate God's 'lower' nature, the manifested world. Those who oppose life's movement are said to be sinful and live in vain (III.16). Instead of forsaking the world established by God, we are called upon to fulfil its purpose by becoming instruments of the Divine Will. We are asked to promote the welfare of the world (*loka-saṃgraha*), by maintaining the order innate in the universe. The wheel of becoming only grinds those who pursue selfish ends. It cannot affect the man who has conquered himself by the Self and whose deeds have become sacrifice

The Buddha does not favour this ideal of inaction in action. His teaching shows a distinct predilection for the life of cessation (*nivṛtti-mārga*). As is evident from numerous passages in the Pāli Canon the Buddha taught that to reach the ultimate goal of *nirvāṇa*, a man had to give up the life of a householder and go forth into homelessness as a mendicant monk. He felt that the obstacles arising from the constant bombardment with objects of pleasure would not allow the mind of a householder to develop the high degree of detachment necessary to realise the goal. The virtuous householder was at best destined to obtain rebirth on a higher, non-human level of existence.

In the *Gītā* this attitude receives a 180° turn. Kṛṣṇa questions the value of the monastic life as a means to emancipation and passionately defends the life of a householder, as best suited to develop a man's wisdom. Once the goal is reached it matters little, whether one abstains from work or continues with an active life. For then, the perfected *yogin* will express the will of the Whole by whatever he does.

Kṛṣṇa distinguishes between the *yogin* who is 'on the way' and the one who has reached the pinnacle of Yoga:

For the sage (*muni*) desiring-to-ascend [to the heights of] Yoga, action is said to be the means. For him who has ascended [to the apex of] Yoga, quiescence (*śama*) is said to be the means. (VI.3)

Śaṅkara and, surprisingly, even Rāmānuja understand 'quiescence' as 'ceasing to act'. This is hardly credible. 'Quiescence' is not an external function. The usage of the word *śama* in the *Gītā* points clearly to its psychological quality. It is inner tranquillity nourished by the realisation of the immanence of God in all things. Another way to explain it would be 'serene openness'. For the *yoga-ārūḍha* or perfected being no further purification is necessary. His one and only purpose is to let the divine light flow through him without disturbing or encroaching upon its course, and to enter into an increasingly deeper relationship with the Whole.

In contrast with the unified state of the emancipated being, the path of the *ārurukṣu* or aspirant is a multiple endeavour with distinct stages of achievement. The yogic path is a gradual unfoldment of our potential. Self-realisation is not within the reach of the weakling. Without diligence and energy no progress can be made. Ignorance has deep roots, and the light of the Supreme Being is covered by many veils. Arjuna realised this:

The mind is fickle, o Kṛṣṇa, impetuous [and] exceedingly strong. Its restraint, I think, is very difficult [to achieve] like [that of] the wind. (VI.34)

To this Kṛṣṇa replied:

Undoubtedly, o strong-armed [Arjuna], the mind is hard-to-seize [and] fickle. But through practice (*abhyāsa*) and dispassion (*vairāgya*), o son-of-Kuntī, it can be seized. (VI.35)

Practice and dispassion are the positive and the negative poles of spiritual life and to be found in every school or system of self-transcendence. Their respective function is explained in the *Yoga-Bhāsya*, the oldest known commentary on the *Yoga-Sūtra* of Patañjali:

The stream of the mind (*citta*) flows both ways; it flows towards the good, and it flows towards the bad. That [stream] which starts with discernment (*viveka*) and which ends in emancipation is the stream of the good. That which starts with non-discernment (*a-viveka*) and which ends in conditioned existence (*saṃsāra*) is the stream to the bad. Through dispassion the streaming out towards wordly objects is checked, and through practice of discerning vision the stream of discernment [leading to emancipation] is laid bare.[63]

Just as dispassion grows with the deepening understanding of what is ephemeral and wherein consists abiding peace and happiness, so practice or *abhyāsa* is a graded effort. It begins with improving one's relationship with other beings. This is done by observing certain basic rules which are common to all forms of religious life. Among these are 'non-hurting' (*ahiṃsā*), 'truthfulness' (*satya*), 'non-coveting' (*aparigraha*) and 'chastity' (*brahmacarya*). In the *Yoga-Sūtra* it is stated that these ought to be practised irrespective of one's social standing, place, time or circumstances.[64] The *Gītā* mentions further 'patience' (*kṣamā*), 'generosity' (*dāna*), 'uprightness' (*ārjava*) and other virtues.[65] Unlike Patañjali, Kṛṣṇa does not distinguish specifically between virtues which are designed to improve interhuman relationships and those which are chiefly meant to raise his inner life.

Life is undivided. The human mind is not an assembly of otherwise independent categories. One cannot really exercise patience with others as long as one does not have control over oneself. Nor can one practise truthfulness without at the same time developing a sense of inner purity. Kindness, forgiveness, concern for others as well as the desire not to hurt either in deed, word or thought, are all founded on inner contentment and strength. Our behaviour merely reflects the condition of our inner life.

Some of the practices for self-improvement mentioned in the *Gītā* are 'purification' (*śauca*), 'asceticism' (*tapas*), 'self-study' (*svādhyāya*) and 'devotion to the Lord' (*īśvara-praṇidhāna*). These are also enlisted by Patañjali. They lead to a more penetrating understanding of human nature and produce the strength required for cultivating all other virtues.

The greatest duty of the householder-*yogin* is to realise that all beings dwell in God and that there is nothing that is not sanctified by His presence. At first this will be no more than an intuitive flash. As he gains greater serenity and lucidity, this spontaneous recognition deepens and widens. When the mist of ignorance and selfishness has cleared from the mirror of his mind through uninterrupted practice, the world becomes transparent to him, and suddenly he sees right into the heart of things.

He [whose] self is yoked in Yoga [and who] everywhere beholds the same, sees the Self abiding in all beings and all beings in the Self. (VI.29)

It is this fulfilling vision of the unity of all beings which is the basis of the attitude of reverence for life which the *Gītā* exacts us to cultivate.

[A man should] not hate any being, [but be] friendly and compassionate, devoid of 'I' [and] 'mine', the same in suffering and pleasure [and] patient. (XII.13)

As the *Īśa-Upaniṣad* (stanza 6) affirms:

But he who beholds all beings in the Self, and the Self in all beings, no longer hates.

In order to climb to these heights of realisation, daily life must become continuous spiritual practice. Once the adverse or, as Kṛṣṇa says, daemoniac tendencies of the mind are subjugated, they must not be given any chance to rise up again. This calls for undiminished attention and effort throughout the day. Our various activities must become offerings to the

Divine, and in everything should we endeavour to fulfil the prompting of the Creator within us. Inner tranquillity is an inevitable prerequisite for our ability to hear God's voice amidst the uproar of secular life.

Hence we must provide for periods of quiet and contemplation, during which we make an intensified effort to open ourselves to the ever-flowing and ever-present creative force of God. The peace and strength acquired during these times especially set aside for introspection should then be tested, put to use and, if possible, enhanced in everyday life. Spiritual power must not be hoarded, but shared.

The *Gītā* contains a few helpful directions about the procedures which ought to be adopted for the practice of meditative absorption (*dhyāna*).

The yogin should continually yoke [him]self [and at set times] remain in privacy, alone, [with] mind and self restrained, without hope [and] not languishing [for objects-of-sense].

Setting up a steady seat for [him]self in a pure place, neither too high nor too low, with a cloth, deer-skin or grass upon it,

there making the mind one-pointed, restraining the activity of mind and senses, he should, seated on the seat, yoke [his self] in Yoga for the purification of the self.

Equable, keeping trunk, head [and] neck motionless [and] steady, gazing [relaxedly] at the tip of the nose, without looking round about him,

[with] tranquil self [and] devoid of fear, steadfast in the vow of celibacy, controlling the mind, [his] thoughts on Me, yoked—he should sit intent on Me. (VI.10–14)

Meditative absorption is the alpha and omega of yogic practice. It is the one-pointed attention to the Divine Being, the opening of our heart to the Silent Ground of existence. *Dhyāna* has to be practised in seclusion. The interminable noise of urban life hardly favours the turning inwards of the mind. Our senses take every opportunity to attach themselves to sound and lure the mind into following their butterfly course.

But the impressions received from the outside world through the senses are not the only impediment which one has to learn to eliminate during absorption. Even when we have become well-nigh oblivious to the external reality and sound and other sense-impressions merely occur as undisturbing phenomena on the periphery of our inner horizon, the powerful mind still continues to cram our consciousness-space (*cid-ākāśa*) with thoughts and seemingly meaningless word configurations. They bubble up from our subconscious mind and are activated mainly by our present worries and preoccupations. Often they start off strong emotional waves which promptly throw us out of the just established inner continuum. Hence Kṛṣṇa's emphasis on the absence of desires and hopes.

Apart from the inner attitude, also the bodily posture is of central importance in guiding the mind inwards. A slack posture will impede the free activity of the lungs and possibly the distribution of the nervous energy. On the other hand, 'erect' posture does not mean 'tense'. Physical relaxation is correlated with the inner ability to let go, and any tension in the body points to a blockage within oneself. This aspect of Yoga has been given almost exclusive attention in Haṭhayoga. Textbooks such as the *Haṭhayoga-Pradīpikā*, *Gheraṇḍa-Saṃhitā* and *Śiva-Saṃhitā* enumerate and describe a great variety of 'postures' called *āsanas* or *pīṭhas*. Some of them are designed to aid meditative absorption. The majority, however, are ingeniously devised techniques for strengthening the body and making it fit for prolonged periods of introspection.

One very revealing fact which emerges from the above description is that Kṛṣṇa, like the later Zen masters, apparently favours absorption with eyes open. The *yogin* is asked to look relaxedly but steadily at the tip of his nose. This direction is not easy to follow. But meditating with closed eyelids always invites sleep, that greatest of obstacles to introspection.

Although the *Gītā* shows acquaintance with techniques for the control of the vital-force (*prāṇa*), it does not enter into a discussion of this important aspect of Yoga practice. There is only one passage in which *prāṇāyāma* is referred to:

Shutting out [all] external contacts and [fixing] the sight between the eyebrows, making even the in-flow and out-flow [of vital-force in the form of breath] moving within the nostrils . . . (V.27)

As scanty as the information given in this stanza is, it is sufficient to reveal the enormous difference between the type of *prāṇāyāma* recommended by Kṛṣṇa and that defined in the *Yoga-Sūtra* of Patañjali. There is no mention here of strenuous retention of breath or remaining in the state of exhalation for an unnaturally long period. Kṛṣṇa simply speaks of 'equalising' inhalation and exhalation. This rhythmisation of breathing corresponds with the dynamic form of absorption advocated in the *Gītā*, and it shows a marked resemblance to certain Buddhist techniques in which mindfulness of breathing is required.

The fact that Kṛṣṇa does not furnish us with precise and detailed instructions about meditation techniques and other auxiliary practices, clearly evinces that he is more concerned with our *inner* attitude during and after introspection rather than with external means of bringing the psycho-mental complex to a relative standstill. Peace and wisdom grow from within. No amount of technical devices of one form or another can replace the inner effort which we have to make in order to rechannel our mind.

A too optimistic reliance on external aids during meditative absorption tends to slacken the will-power and wakeful attention in workaday life. Instead we should regard the 're-tuning' of the mind as a task which is before us all the time and not only during the spells of creative withdrawal. Life must become an uninterrupted self-offering to God.

Whatever you do, whatever you eat, whatever you sacrifice, whatever you give away, whatever austerities [you may practise]—do that, o son-of-Kuntī, as an offering (*arpaṇa*) to Me.

Kṛṣṇa's Yoga aims straight at the realisation of the Self without long detours through intermediate goals. It neither encourages the acquisition of magical powers (*siddhis*) nor the practice of lower states of enstasis (*samādhi*). Its one and only object is the recovery of the Self as a 'particle' of the all-engirdling body of God. Hence meditative absorption is not contemplation of this or that object, but primarily God-mindedness —a wholehearted turning of oneself to the light which abides in the heart.

Of all the *yogins*, he who loves Me [with his] inner self absorbed in Me—him I deem to be most yoked. (VI.47)

For those men who, reflecting on Me [with] undiverted [mind], love [Me] ever full-yoked—I hold out security in Yoga. (IX.22)

This brings us to the devotional (*bhakti*) element in Kṛṣṇa's Yoga. We have seen how the *Gītā* combines and, in fact, integrates wisdom (*jñāna*) and action (*karman*). What place does it assign in its grand synthesis to love? The following stanza contains in a nutshell Kṛṣṇa's exceptional point of view:

That Supreme Being, o son-of-Pṛthā, is to be won by love (*bhakti*) [directed to] none other. In Him all beings abide, by Him this whole [universe] is spread out [like a spider's web]. (VIII.22)

The word *bhakti* is derived from the root √*bhaj* 'to participate in', and it designates a loving participation in God's all-pervasive Being. But *bhakti* also stands for God's love of man, as this verse bears out:

Just as these [*yogins*] approach Me, so do I love them [in turn]. Everywhere, o son-of-Pṛthā, men follow My 'track'. (IV.11)

The *Gītā* recognises two stages or degrees of love. The one is the ordinary devotion of the pious *yogin* towards the Divine Essence; the other is the relationship of love-participation realised with his attainment of emancipation. This supreme love (*parā-bhakti*) is perfect union which gives content and meaning to liberation. This is the great novelty of Kṛṣṇa's doctrine.

It is not enough to prevent the mind from pursuing worldly pleasures and render it still by diligently guarding the five 'gates' of the senses. Its natural inclination will drive it back outwards into the mundane 'field' (*kṣetra*) as soon as the reins of self-discipline are even slightly released. Detachment creates an inner vacuum which by its very nature attracts things into it. Hence considerable effort is needed to sustain it for any length of time. Thus in order to rid ourselves of all attachment to transient objects, we are told to artificially create a state of voidness within us which will gradually 'freeze' the natural tendency of the mind to flow out through the senses.

Kṛṣṇa suggests a different, and it seems more natural, way. He does not condemn attachment as such, which is merely a directedness of the mind. His only concern is the object to which the mind clings. Since attachment to mundane things leads to self-alienation, only one way remains to fulfil the call of our 'essential nature'. And this is to attach our mind to God and let ourselves be carried along the vigorous ascending current which begins and terminates in Him. Thus, instead of dissipating the mind's power by permitting it to run after so many objects of sense, we must concentrate it and channel it towards the Supreme Being. We must melt our innumerable desires into one all-powerful urge upwards.

This love for God is non-distinct from wisdom and creative action. It is the eternal interplay of creativity within the incommensurable Whole. Love intensifies as wisdom grows and it, in turn, suffuses wisdom with life. Action fortifies love, and love enriches action. Kṛṣṇa's Yoga restores and safeguards the wholeness of Man's nature. No aspect of man is denied or belittled. Each is being attuned to the other. The resultant harmonisation is the bed-rock on which is founded the ultimate perfection of man, the disowning of the self and immediate revelation of the Self dwelling in God.

VI. THE ETHICS OF KṚṢṆA*

Today, we witness a widespread disillusionment about traditional moral standards. We are no longer receptive to the fixed, authoritarian ethical models of our forefathers. The idea of god-kings or deified priests embodying Divine Right seems deplorable to us. The promise of Heaven and the agonies of Hell no longer have a threatening power over our imagination.

We sense a twisted idealism in the eighteenth-century doctrine of Natural Right, and the attempt of the nineteenth-century materialists to abstract a basis for ethics from the Darwinian theory of the survival of the fittest (not necessarily the best), seems equally distorted. We are weary and impatient with absolutistic ethics. Our values and outlook on life have unsettled rapidly during the post-war years.

But we have not yet crystallised the new values and attitudes which have grown in us. The present-day non-committal libertinism and permissiveness are not finalised solutions. Strictly speaking, they are no more than the coefficients of a phase of fundamental change—merely emotional reactions to our severance from the old world. We face today the formidable and imperative task of having to identify and assemble the

*In this chapter I venture to touch on the tender subject of the constellation of a new life-style which is about to supersede the run-down mental-dualistic thought form which we inherited from the nineteenth century. The fact that the present-day global crisis involves something as fundamental as the emergence of a new mode of *consciousness* was first pointed out with full force by the Swiss cultural philosopher Jean Gebser in his monumental study *Ursprung und Gegenwart* (Stuttgart, 1949–53). About the same time Srī Aurobindo in the East and Teilhard de Chardin in the West independently expressed a similar conviction.

many insights, impressions and anticipatory feelings belonging to the new world, into a harmonious and coherent whole. A new ethics will have to emerge which can measure up to the changed internal and external conditions of contemporary life.

It would be unwise to forecast in detail the nature of this forming ethics. However, its general character can be anticipated to a certain extent. We might safely assume that it will *not* be lop-sided absolutistic, autocratic, idealistic, naturalistic, evolutionistic, opportunistic, individualistic or socialistic. In contrast, it will be integrative and will fully respect the holistic nature of man.

A glimpse of what this might involve can be obtained from modern jurisprudence, for example, when Hans Marti, Professor of Constitutional Law at Berne University, presses that the law should present 'a picture of the whole world'.[66]

The reader may now ask what role the archaic teaching of Kṛṣṇa can possibly play in this crucial phase of transition from the inflexible ethics of the terminating mental-perspectivic life-style to the *open* ethics of the advancing a-rational (not irrational!) integral mode of being. The answer is simply that the *Gītā* can today serve as a reliable sign-post and inestimable starting-point for our individual self-finding and orientation in a world of crisis and confusion. Let it be stated quite clearly that I do not assert that the ethics of the *Gītā* necessarily coincides fully with the *open* ethics of the coming age. But I do most positively affirm that the dialogue between Kṛṣṇa and Arjuna offers certain fundamental reflections and elementary practical solutions which can promote our personal endeavour to crystallise in ourselves the new *Zeitgeist*.

It is beyond the scope of this book to give an exhaustive presentation of this topic. What is possible within the present context is to give a clear statement of the fundamental issues involved and perhaps make some constructive suggestions. It has been said of the Greek epics that they offend our sense of justice. This may be so. However, when the great Indian saga of Vyāsa, the *Mahābhārata*, is charged with advocating a derelict morality, I must come to its defence. Hopefully, the following sketch should annul further denunciations or unjust attacks on Hindu morality and render them meaningless.

Religion is said to be concerned with the relationship of man to a superhuman reality, and ethics, in contrast, is the relationship between man and man and other sentient beings. However, ethics cannot be dissociated from man's attitude towards the superhuman reality, or, for that matter, from his attitude towards Nature and life in general. A rigid compartmentalisation of man's relationships would be completely out of place and, in fact, is one of the causes responsible for the failure of most Western ethical systems.

Ethics must be based on an integral picture of man. This is brought out quite clearly in Kṛṣṇa's wisdom-doctrine. He has steered clear of the serious fallacy of most other ethical thinkers, namely to over-emphasise certain aspects of man's nature and neglect or completely ignore the rest. In its ethics, the *Gītā* attempts to reflect the whole human being. Hence its standpoint is profoundly complex.

It is self-evident that the reflections put forward in this chapter are unlikely to have entered the mind of the author of the *Gītā* in the same form. Vyāsa belonged to an age in which prevailed what Jean Gebser styled the *mythic* structure of consciousness. This pictorial-introvertive consciousness operated with its own specific set of symbols to express man's insights and experiences. However, it must not be forgotten that Vyāsa's work is the culmination of a long process of profound philosophical and ethical thinking.[67]

Ethics tries to answer the question: What must we do in order to realise what is right and good. It is the theory of morality. Hence ethics is essentially evaluation. It is founded on an appraisal of reality, and therefore is intimately bound up with metaphysics. Since metaphysics depends on man's varying capacity of understanding, there is not one ethics but a great variety of ethical systems or models, some of which are totally incompatible.

Principally, ethics may assume either of two forms. It can be heteronomous or autonomous. In the former case, the moral law which it advocates is unquestionable and fixed by authority of one kind or another. An instance in point are the ten commandments which God is said to have revealed to Moses. Autonomous ethics, on the other hand, is man-made. A host of divergent systems can be distinguished, and spearheading the contemporary ethical field are the sociological and the existentialist approaches.

The widely accepted 'sociological' theory of value is that human values are agreed upon by the members of a society for the benefit of society. According to this model, conscience is merely the product of the demands made by society on its individual members. In other words, ethics is approached from a purely utilitarian angle and the question of 'meaning' does not enter at all. This view offers a merely quantitative appraisal of man: Good is what best serves most people. It overthrows the value of the individual who is indirectly encouraged not to accept full ethical responsibility. The result is that conscience is being projected on to the larger group. This approach overlooks the fact that it is the individual human being who makes up society. We are ourselves first before we are anything else. The individual's lack of interest in ethical responsibility will, when promoted by an unrealistic theory of value, ultimately destroy society itself.

In contradistinction to this anti-individualistic attitude stands the existentialist view that each man's values must be his own. The best known advocate of this type of ethics is Jean-Paul Sartre. His principal argument is that because we ourselves are responsible for creating our values, we are free to act in any way whatsoever, as long as we do it out of free choice. Sartre does not shy away from the extreme that if a person chose to murder and steal or turned to any other vice, there would be no wrong in that: Right is, what is in accord with one's free choice. This strikes a false note, to say the least. It ends in a complete relativisation of all values. And this is Nihilism which Sartre, with sinister indifference, asks us to accept courageously.

Logical as this conclusion is within Sartre's philosophical system, it is based on a profound metaphysical blunder. Sartre thinks that man is *radically* free. He prefers to ignore the fact that the past influences and shapes life in the present. Conveniently, he denies the existence of the subliminal strata of consciousness, thus going against the momentous findings of Psychology.

This radical freedom is a myth. First of all, man is not a disembodied mind. He is part of Nature and hence has to obey certain laws. Even if we were to opt against the law of gravity, we would not actually achieve anything positive by our disagreement. Furthermore, if we wish to stay alive, we *must* breathe and nourish our body; if we omit to do so, we will die *against* our will. To oppose Nature is to inflict suffering and restriction on us, and that is tantamount to the curtailment of our free will. Wherein then does our radical freedom lie?

It is clear from what has been said so far that human values are not arbitrary creations. There is a frame of reference in nature which, when ignored, has detrimental effects on the person who, knowingly or not, has transgressed Nature's laws. On the other hand, it is equally evident from everyday life that man is, to a certain degree, free to choose *within* this objective framework. This is the precise standpoint of Kṛṣṇa.

One may next ask whether this objective frame of reference can be made a base of ethical thinking. Can one deduct an absolute moral law from Nature as we know it through our senses? Perhaps this would be possible, if both Nature and human will were governed exclusively by determinism. This is definitely not the case with man. And modern science has reached a stage when it begins to question quite seriously determinism in Nature as well. Nature is not a closed continuum, but an open order. 'Forces of spirit may break upon it and change its course'.[68] Nature as the physical 'environment' presented to our sense-organs is but the outermost surface of a multi-dimensional structure, the roots of which reach down into the very ground of being. In the words of Kṛṣṇa, it subsists in God, the all-pervasive Being.

If we were to extract *absolute* values from the data of this surface-reality, we would be badly misled. Because Nature does not follow an entirely deterministic pattern, but is open, life is to a large extent unpredictable. Therefore we cannot use our actions as measures of moral right or wrong. This has induced Kant to look within man for some kind of standard by which one could scale the morality or immorality of an action. He found it in the categorical imperative supplied by reason. The question here is whether absolute values can be considered to work unconditionally at all times in the relative sphere of life. If we, as Kant demands, orientate ourselves for the rightfulness or wrongfulness of our deeds purely on our motives or intentions and disregard the outcome of our actions, this can lead to real anomalies in practical life. One cannot help concluding that abstract absolute values cannot be applied absolutely. Intention and resultant action cannot be separated. Kant fell prey to dualism, that unavoidable corollary of rationality pushed to the extreme. At the same time, one also cannot maintain the converse idea that the outcome of a deed outweighs the initiatory intention. For example, somebody intends to hurt by his action, but by some unforeseen intervening circumstance this results in the saving of human life. Does this make the action moral? Surely not.

The fact that absolute moral standards have been found not to work unconditionally in actual life does not mean a return to the nihilistic standpoint favoured by Sartre and others. For, denial of the absoluteness of abstract moral laws does not do away with the objective foundation of ethical values. It is a fatal misconception to think that moral order and reason must be identical. Similarly it is ill-conceived, of course, to deny values altogether. There are no absolutely right decisions, just as there is no absolute free will. Categorical imperatives are outdated.

The middle path, taught by Kṛṣṇa, is the relativity (not subjectivity!) of values. Life is not abstract. It is always a specific case, a particular situation involving particular individuals.

The exclusive reliance on reason for answering ethical questions has proven a pitfall to Western philosophers. Reason works with abstraction, not the 'concretes' of life. It represents a static picture or 'cross-section' of reality. The pioneers of the intellect are beginning to realise this. More and more, scientists call for a complete overhaul of scientific methodology. The criteria of validity are shifting perceptibly from 'abstract' and 'consistent' to 'practical workability'.

It is exactly this empirical-experimental rationale which is at the bottom of the Eastern schools of thought, particularly in the area of ethics. Indian ethics, as exemplified in the *Gītā*, does not put the same unreserved, almost naïve trust in reason as its Western counterpart. The diversified processes of life cannot be abstracted by reason and retain at the same time their 'life' quality. An ethics grounded in pure generalisations cannot possibly be expected to answer any practical purposes. Therefore Kṛṣṇa founds his ethics on a deeper and wider understanding of life. He does not discard reason, but he also does not rely on it. His attitude is refreshingly experiential: Life itself must be the ultimate criterion of the applicability of ethical ideals.

Indian ethics necessarily emphasises the individual as the primary concrete principle of human life. But it is not anti-social, as has so often been assumed in a summary fashion. Its true position is expressed in a well-known Sanskrit aphorism: For the family sacrifice the individual; for the community the family; for the country the community—and for the Self (*ātman*) the whole world. Judged by cold reason this seems utterly tautological. Since the realisation of the Self depends on the individual's efforts, how can the individual be said to be subordinate to the family, group or the whole of mankind? This is one of the many examples of the innate resistance of the Indian mind to assume an arid, purely dualistic attitude towards life. It rejects the rationalistic 'either-or' schematism and replaces it with an admittedly paradoxical but true-to-life attitude which knows of an 'as well as'.

Ethical evaluation depends on inner principles as much as on objective factors. Hence both need to be taken into account in ethical life. In the *Gītā* a stupendous effort is made to give an integral interpretation of reality, whereby ethics and metaphysics are not anxiously kept apart.

This meaningful ambivalence is also preserved in the key concept of Kṛṣṇa's ethical teachings—*dharma*. This word has suffered a great many misinterpretations. Terms like 'virtue', 'righteousness' or even 'religion' have habitually been employed in translation, but none of these renderings connotes the full meaning of the Sanskrit word. *Dharma*, from √*dhṛ* 'to hold, bear', is used in the classical literature of India in an abundant variety of ways. Consequently it depends entirely on the context how this term should best be translated. In Buddhist scriptures alone, seven distinct usages of *dharma* can be distinguished.[69] For example, it denotes the 'doctrine' of the Buddha, the 'ultimate principles' into which he analysed the cosmic flux, the 'order' which exists in the universe and the 'transcendental reality' itself.

Two principal meanings of *dharma* can be made out. It stands for the 'universal harmony' which is identical with man's essential being, and it represents the 'ethical norm' by which this essential being is actualised. The latter is defined in the *Mahābhārata* (III.32.22–4) thus:

> *Dharma* is the bark: there is no other for men who go to heaven. It is the ship that ferries the merchant to the other side of the ocean. For if *dharma* performed by men who live the life of *dharma* were to go unrewarded, this world would be submerged in darkness without basis or support. None would draw nigh to *Nirvāṇa* and men would lead the life of beasts. They would be struck down and never attain any object.[70]

Dharma thus appears as a particularisation on the human level of the supreme order prevailing in the universe, the 'lower nature' of God. This cosmic harmony, also called *ṛta* in the Vedas, is manifest in

> the spontaneous rightness observable in the majestic movement of the stars, the recurrence of the seasons, the unswerving alternance of day and night, the unerring rhythm of birth, growth, death . . .[71]

Only when man has realised within himself this universal order can he be said to have fulfilled the individual moral 'norm' or *dharma*.[72] Selfish interests which taint our view of reality blind us to the fact that the individual human law is contained in the larger cosmic order. However, actions which are rooted in *dharma* help to establish harmony within ourselves and by so doing promote the process of Self-realisation. The high road to emancipation (*mokṣa-mārga*) is inseparable from the path of moral norm (*dharma-mārga*).

In the *Gītā*, *dharma* does not play the role of an infallible categorical imperative. Kṛṣṇa's ethics is opposed to the formalism of the Mīmāṃsā school of thought according to which the moral law consists in a strict adherence to the injunctions found in the Vedas. He does not believe that scriptural precepts are a sufficient guide to consummate *dharma*. For example, the leading Mīmāṃsā thinker Kumārila enjoins the performance of the magical *śyena*-sacrifice mentioned in the Vedas, irrespective of its evil consequences for those against whom it is directed and for the sacrificer himself. Rightly Kṛṣṇa discourages this kind of totally unenlightened legalistic attitude.

For this reason one must also reject S. N. Dasgupta's interpretation of *dharma* as 'unalterable customary order of class-duties or caste-duties and the general approved course of conduct'.[73] This stresses too much the external or social implications of *dharma* and entirely ignores its profound metaphysical and psychological significance. In Dasgupta's opinion the 'individual norm' (*sva-dharma*) refers merely to the duties laid down by tradition for each of the four castes. This is only conditionally correct. We have seen that originally the caste system was based on an analysis of man's differing psychological make-up, and that the *Gītā* still knows of and respects this differentiation of human types on psychological grounds.

It would be more appropriate to interpret *sva-dharma* as 'innate law' or even 'law of active self-determination'. *Sva-dharma* is the 'ought' which our essential being (*sva-bhāva*) presents to the mind in order that it can fulfil itself. In other words, *sva-dharma* is the channel through which man can reach his essential nature, that is, realise his 'innate idea'. It has far more in common with Socrates' inner voice, the *daimonion*, than with moral obligations embodied in certain rules. Kṛṣṇa says:

Better is [one's] own norm imperfectly [carried out] than another's norm well-performed . . . (III.35[a])

Nevertheless, it would be quite erroneous to assume that Kṛṣṇa dispenses with all authority. For those who have not yet attained to the moral 'conscience' or awareness which coincides with the awakening of the wisdom-faculty (*buddhi*), there are mainly two external 'standards' by which they can determine the moral quality of a deed. These are the example set by great men and the prevalent traditional moral code. However, Kṛṣṇa does not advocate blind faith in either of the two. Instead, he recommends the intuitive and, not least, rational valuation of one's actions.

Kṛṣṇa's commendation to renounce the 'fruit' (*phala*) of one's actions does not imply a disavowal of the value of deliberation over the consequences of one's deeds, as some interpreters of the *Gītā* have held. The term *phala* is not synonymous with 'consequence'. Rather it refers to the 'psychic tension' in our actions, that is, the ego-centred anticipations we harbour while performing actions. Kṛṣṇa asks us not to work for the sake of personal reward. This, again, must not be misconstrued to mean 'duty for duty's sake'. Kṛṣṇa does not deny us the joy arising from a proper and successful active life. He only insists that we should abandon our *selfish* desires (*kāma*) and attachments. Acts can be of a triple nature according to the prevalence of either of the three types of *guṇas*.

[That] work which is incumbent [and which is] done without attachment [and] without passion [or] hatred by [one who] craves not for the fruit [of action]—that is called *sattva* [-natured].

But the action which is done with great strain by [one who] craves [to realise selfish] desires or else out of self-sense (*ahaṃkāra*)—that is named *rajas* [-natured].

[That] action which is undertaken through delusion, without regard to the consequence, [be it] loss or hurt, [or] to the human-capacity (*pauruṣa*)—that is called *tamas* [-natured]. (XVIII.23–5)

The renunciation of the fruit of one's deed does not mean complete disinterest in the outcome of one's action. Kṛṣṇa has in mind a much more positive attitude towards work. Actions are never to be carried out thoughtlessly. And it betrays a complete lack of reflection to assume, as some modern interpreters of the *Gītā* have done, that Kṛṣṇa wants us to abandon all motives. Actions are impossible without some kind of motivation behind them. Kṛṣṇa only demands that our deeds become more and more unselfish, and that we should endeavour to heed the sustenance of others and promote their well-being by our acts. This must not be misunderstood as an exhortation to adopt a self-destructive altruism. He does not commend us to work for the pleasure of others, but rather for their good, which is what is conducive to Self-realisation. The implication is that the true good of others is also our own good, because both converge in the Self. Kṛṣṇa's social ideal is expressed in the concept of *loka-saṃgraha* or 'bringing together of the world'.

Our acts must not only be performed with the proper inner attitude, but they must also be right in themselves.

Therefore, always unattached, perform the *right* deed . . . (III.19)

The word *kārya*, translated here with 'right', actually means 'to be done'. Right is what is to be done, because convention, reason and deeper insight demand it. For, does not Kṛṣṇa, towards the end of his discourse (XVIII.63), bid Arjuna to reflect (*vimṛśya*) carefully on the secret doctrine he has expounded to him—and then choose a course of action? The adoption of an unselfish attitude does not release us from the responsibility of acting *rightly*. It is not enough that we do away with such negative emotions as hatred or greed and that we renounce all egotistic intentions; we must also pay undivided attention to the intrinsic rightness or wrongness of an action, and decide to the best of our knowledge.

However, Kṛṣṇa is realistic enough not to believe in an absolute right or wrong. They are not so much opposites than interacting poles. It is polarity which informs the universe.

All actions should be performed in a spirit of equability (*samatva*). This 'same-ness' is the mainstay of Kṛṣṇa's Yoga. This must not be misinterpreted as a mechanical indifference towards everything. It is a positive state of mind in which we are able to look with balanced serenity on all the many things that would ordinarily upset us and stir up unwholesome emotions and becloud our judgement. *Samatva* does not necessitate the eradication of feeling, as has been widely assumed by misinformed adherents of Buddhism. Nothing could be more alien to the world-affirming character of the *Gītā* than to demand of us aridity of feeling and complete apathy to objects of beauty. Neither does it demand disinterest in manifestations of the truth, the right and the good.

Sound moral conduct furthers the emergence of the wisdom-faculty (*buddhi*). When true wisdom arises, our actions become grounded in the universal order (*ṛta*) embedded in the depths of our being. At that moment the *yogin* crosses the threshold of contingent existence and transcends all good and bad. He then realises in full the ideal of inaction-in-action. His path becomes the divine course itself, which seeks fulfilment through him.

[The *yogin*] does not rejoice on gaining a beloved [object] nor does he become agitated on encountering unpleasant [things]. Having steadied the wisdom-faculty the knower-of-*brahman*, devoid of confusion, abides in *brahman*. (V.20)

VII. THE GOAL: EMANCIPATION AS SELF-AWAKENING IN GOD

The Yoga of the *Gītā* differs, as we have seen, from other forms of Yoga both in its theoretical presuppositions and its methodological approach. In view of this remarkable fact it is surprising that so few students of the *Gītā* have failed to notice the uniqueness of Kṛṣṇa's conception of emancipation (*mokṣa*). This is probably due to the widespread but ill-conceived notion that the experience of self-transcending illumination is a uniform phenomenon. The illegitimacy of this view was conclusively demonstrated by R. C. Zaehner, who made a special study of this vital question.[74] He distinguished three basic types of what he called 'praeternatural experience':

(i) The apperception of the unity underlying the multiplicity of Nature, usually coupled with a pantheistic conception of reality.
(ii) The realisation of the ground of the inner being of man, based on a monistic philosophy.
(iii) The experience of Self-awakening in God, linked to a pan-en-theistic metaphysics.

The unitive life of the Indian mystics or *yogins* is predominantly of the first type of experience of all-in-one, for which R. C. Zaehner coined the term *pan-en-henism*. The classic mystical formula 'I am the world-ground' (*ahaṃ brahma-asmi*) best exemplifies this widely attested experience. Paradigmatic of the second type is the end-state of Classical Yoga and Sāṃkhya. Here emancipation is experienced as a total 'isolation' (*kaivalya*) from the world and perfect, 'hermetic', immersion into the transcendental Self-monad. The first type leaves God out altogether or reduces Him to the role of a unifying principle in Nature; the second merely looks inwards into the human soul identifying the inmost Self with God. Those who pursue Self-realisation apart from God are compared, in the *Yatīndramata-Dīpikā* of Śrīnivāsadāsa, to women deserted by their husbands. Neither experience is characteristic of the ultimate goal advocated by Kṛṣṇa.

For him God is not merely world-ground or soul-ground. He *is* in His own right. Nature and Self, *prakṛti* and *puruṣa*, have their being in Him. He is their essence and yet is not circumscribed by them. Consequently emancipation takes place *within* His unfathomable profundity. This proposition is borne out by numerous stanzas in the *Gītā*.

That man who, having forsaken all desires, moves about devoid of longing, devoid of [the thought of] 'mine', without ego-sense—he approaches peace (*śānti*). (II.71)

This is the state of *brahman*, o son-of-Pṛthā. Attaining this [a man] is no [longer] deluded. Abiding therein also at the end-time [i.e. at death], he attains extinction-in-*brahman*. (II.72)

He who has inner joy, inner rejoicing, and inner light is a *yogi*. Having become *brahman*, he approaches extinction-in-*brahman*. (V.24)

Thus ever yoking the self, the *yogin* of restrained mind approaches peace, the supreme extinction (*nirvāṇa*) [which] subsists in Me. (VI.15)

He who is intent on oneness (*ekatva*) [and] loves Me, abiding in all beings, in whatever [state] he exists—that *Yogin* dwells in Me. (VI.31)

From this it is evident that Kṛṣṇa recognises two degrees or stages of emancipation. The first is the more common mystical experience of oneness with Nature, when the *yogin* beholds the Self in all beings and all beings in the Self. This state is also referred to as 'having become *brahman*'. It is the Self-finding in the world-ground, 'the extinction-in-*brahman*'.[75] But this fixed, still state of extinction (*nirvāṇa*) is not a totally unconditioned mode of being. It is said to subsist in God. Therefore the *yogin* must not delude himself into thinking that this is the termination of his inward journey.

Having achieved identification with the world-ground, another and far greater challenge awaits the *yogin*. He is now free to discover the foundation of the All, the infinite living God. In a last act of self-surrender, the liberated being must open himself to the eternal love of God. Wisdom (*jñāna*) has helped him to cross over the ocean of conditioned existence and transcend space and time—now love (*bhakti*) must unite him to the Supreme Being.

Kṛṣṇa is explicit on this point:

Of all *yogins*, he who loves Me with faith [and whose] inner self is absorbed in Me—Him I deem to be most yoked. (VI.47)

The *yogin* can choose between two distinct approaches in order to attain emancipation of the lower type. Either he sets out to discover his essence, the Self, whilst relying on his own innate strength, or else he calls for help from the Divine Being. In both cases, however, he must open himself to an order of life higher than his empirical personality. In the latter approach he makes use of the powerful human capacity for love. The inner vacuum which is created by his turning away from worldly pursuits, is now filled with a truly prodigious power which assists him in overcoming even the strongest resistance of the mind to being transmuted into pure consciousness and thereby transcending the boundaries of the spatio-temporal universe. The divine grace (*prasāda*) of Puruṣottama safely guards the devotee across the chasms of mundane life into the supreme abode of the Lord.

S. Radhakrishnan is wrong when he assumes that Kṛṣṇa maintains two *conflicting* views about the nature of the ultimate perfection.[76] The *Gītā* is quite unequivocal on this point: Conscious communion with God in his eternal *milieu* is infinitely superior to the immobile state of identification with the world-ground.

The devotion cultivated by the *yogin* towards God during

his spiritual ascent is an excellent preparatory for the spontaneous love-participation within God—the 'nerve fluid' running through all the cells of the Divine Organism. The *yogin* who neglects to orientate himself towards the Whole not only renders his path more difficult,[77] but also retrenches the wholeness and grandeur of his state of emancipation. On attaining liberation, he is like a cell awakened to its own existence, but still unconscious of its larger environment.

It is self-evident that the love pulsating in the divine body of God is not of an emotional or intellectual nature. The love that flourishes eternally between God and the Self-particles who have awakened to His presence is one of ineffable divine creativity: The Whole communing with Itself. The logical mind shrinks back from this paradox. It fails to gain a foothold in that realm in which all opposites coincide. The ultimate test must be unmediated experience. This transcendental love (*parā-bhakti*) is an essential part of God and can be fully realised only in and through God. This love is of the *nir-guṇa* type: It is beyond the scope of the primary-constituents of the world. It is unconditional and without object.

Emancipation depends on God. No amount of self-effort can bring about the final fruit of self-transcendence. We must release all tension within us and relinquish our self-will and become still. God's great work can only be accomplished when the soul has become tranquil (*prasāda*). Then we are able to open ourselves to the divine omnipresence. This is true *bhakti* which gives birth to the grace (*prasāda*) of God.

> A man can offer God nothing dearer than peace. God cares not and needs not waking, fasting, praying and all castigation as opposed to peace. God needs nothing more than that one offers Him a calm heart: then he acts such secret and divine works in the soul that no creature can help or even witness them.[78]

Emancipation, both as identification with the world-ground or, in its higher form, as unalloyed union with God, does not end our physical existence abruptly, nor does it prolong our life *ad infinitum*. But it brings meaning and fulfilment to our existence. Liberation renders the world diaphanous. Wherever our glance falls, we behold the Whole, and the Whole holds us. Then we realise that conditioned existence (*saṃsāra*) and the unconditioned mode of being are not opposites. No one has expressed this sublime realisation more comprehensibly than Meister Eckehart:

> Listen to the wonder! How wonderful: to stand outside as well as in, to grasp and be grasped, to look on and at the same time be seen oneself, to hold and be held—that is the aim.[79]

NOTES TO TEXT, APPENDICES, BIBLIOGRAPHY, INDEX

NOTES TO TEXT

Introduction

1. S. Radhakrishnan, *Indian Philosophy*, volume I (London, repr. 1951), p. 66
2. See *Ṛgveda* X.90
3. See *Ṛgveda* X.129
4. *Ṛgveda* I.89
5. *Ṛgveda* X.133.6
6. *Chāndogya-Upaniṣad* VIII.4.1–2
7. *Muṇḍaka-Upaniṣad* II.2.3–4
8. *Bṛhadāraṇyaka-Upaniṣad* IV.4.20–1
9. *Muṇḍaka-Upaniṣad* III.2.9
10. *Viveka-Cūḍāmaṇi*, verses 228 and 230
11. See *Mahābhārata* XII.260
12. See *Mahābhārata* XII.65.24–5; I.106.4–6
13. S. Radhakrishnan, *Indian Philosophy*, volume I, p. 521
14. Aurobindo, *Essays on the Gita* (New York, 1950), p. 5
15. K. N. Upadhyaya, *Early Buddhism and the Bhagavadgītā* (Delhi, 1971), p. 29
16. See G. S. Khair, *Quest for the Original Gita* (Bombay, 1969)
17. K. N. Upadhyaya, *op.cit.*, pp. 10–11
18. Admittedly, there are some works of a philosophical nature, like the *Sāṃkhya-Kārikā* of Īśvara Kṛṣṇa or the *Bodhicaryāvatāra* of Śāntideva, which are composed in verse
19. J. Mascaró, *The Bhagavad Gita*, Penguin Classics (Harmondsworth, 1962), p. 23, (hardcase edition, Rider & Co)
20. S. N. Dasgupta, *A History of Indian Philosophy*, volume II (Cambridge, 1965), p. 534
21. Max Müller, *The Six Systems of Indian Philosophy* (London, repr. 1916), p. 1
22. See *Mahābhārata* I.63
23. *Bhagavad-Gītā* XVIII.75
24. Nataraja Guru, *The Bhagavad Gita* (London, 1961), p. 24
25. S. Radhakrishnan, *op.cit.*, volume I, pp. 521–2
26. Aurobindo, *Essays on the Gita*, p. 7

27. Aurobindo, *The Foundation of Indian Culture* (New York, 1953), pp. 323–4
28. Aurobindo, *op.cit.*, p. 326
29. There is a symbolic component in this for which a possible key might be found in the *Bṛhadāraṇyaka-Upaniṣad* (I.3.1) where we read that the offspring of the Primal Being (Prajāpati) was twofold: gods (*deva*) and demons (*āsura*)—whereby the latter are said to have been far more numerous than the former
30. S. Radhakrishnan, *The Bhagavadgītā* (London, 1948), p. 28
31. *Chāndogya-Upaniṣad* III.17.4
32. *Chāndogya-Upaniṣad* III.17.6
33. See *Mahābhārata* V.48
34. See *Mahābhārata* XII.312.10–12
35. See *Chāndogya-Upaniṣad* I.5.6
36. P. Tillich, 'Theology and Symbolism', *Religious Symbolism*, ed. by F. E. Johnson (New York, 1955), p. 109
37. See *Mahābhārata* I.1
38. See O. Stein, 'The Numeral 18', *Poona Orientalist*, **I**, 3 (Oct. 1936), pp. 1–37; and: 'Additional Notes on the Numeral 18', *Poona Orientalist*, **II**, 3 (Oct. 1937), pp. 164–5
39. *Cf.* Hegel: God dies a thousandfold in the process of cosmic creation and history
40. *Brahmá*, the creative principle, must not be confused with *brahman* which is the ultimate substratum of the universe, i.e. the *ens realissimum*
41. *Taittirīya-Upaniṣad* III.2. *Cf. Mahābhārata* III.208.28: 'Is it not self-evident that fish preys upon fish?'
42. *Taittirīya-Upaniṣad* III.10.6
43. The fourteen instruments (*indriya*) are: the five conative senses plus 'energy' (*bala*) and the five cognitive senses plus the lower mind (*manas*) as well as recollection (*citta*) and the wisdom-faculty (*buddhi*)
44. The three 'states' (*bhāva*) are the efficacies of the three primary-constituents (*guṇa*) of the world-ground
45. The 'embodied' or 'body-bearer' (*dehin*) refers to the individualised Self
46. *Mahābhārata* XII.267.28 (Sukthankar's ed.)

Essential Doctrines

1. E. Swedenborg, Apocalypse Explained, no. 1126
2. E. Swedenborg, True Christian Religion, no. 30
3. *pūrṇam-adaḥ pūrṇam-idaṃ pūrṇāt-pūrṇam-udacyate, pūrṇasya pūrṇam-ādāya pūrṇam-eva-avaśiṣyate.*
4. Plato, *Laws*, 716
5. *Bhagavad-Gītā* IV.6

6. Probably the female principle, later on called *prakṛti*
7. The male principle
8. I follow here A. Hillebrandt's interpretation of *īśa-avāsya* as 'cast upon the lord', from √*as* 'to cast, throw', instead of √*vas* 'to envelop'. See A. Hillebrandt, *Upanishaden: Altindische Weisheit* (Jena, 1964)
9. R. C. Zaehner, *The Bhagavad-Gītā* (Oxford, 1969), pp. 39–40
10. This term is fully analysed in R. C. Zaehner, *op.cit.*, pp. 214–15
11. A. W. Watts, *Psychotherapy East and West* (New York, 1963), p. 21
12. *Mahābhārata* XII.350.60
13. Meister Eckehart, Sermon 33 (Quint's ed.)
14. See *Māṇḍūkya-Kārikā* IV.72
15. See *Bhagavad-Gītā* XV.1
16. This term appears to have been introduced by the Zen-orientated psychotherapist K. Graf von Dürckheim, 'Psychotherapie, Initiation, Glaube', *Abendländische Therapie und östliche Weisheit*, ed. by W. Bitter (Stuttgart, 1968), pp. 16–50
17. See *Bhagavad-Gītā* VII.4–5
18. See *Bhagavad-Gītā* VII.6
19. R. C. Zaehner, *op.cit.*, p. 9
20. Meister Eckehart, Sermon 26 (Quint's ed.)
21. *Kaṭha-Upaniṣad* III.3.–4[a]
22. Quoted in H. C. Warren, *Buddhism in Translation*, Harvard Oriental Series, volume III (Cambridge, Mass., 1906[4]), pp. 131–2
23. *Brahma-Sūtra-Bhāṣya* III.2.16
24. *Katha-Upaniṣad* IV.1[a]
25. Plotinus, *Enneads* ? ? ? (A. H. Armstrong's transl.). *Cf.* Wordsworth:

    We are laid asleep
    In body, and become a living soul;
    While with an eye made quiet by the power
    Of harmony, and the deep power of joy,
    We see into the life of things

26. For a complete translation of this hymn together with a detailed commentary see G. Feuerstein & J. Miller, *A Reappraisal of Yoga* (London, 1971), pp. 64–85
27. The Sanskrit word *aikṣata* (from √*īkṣ* 'to see') is usually translated with 'it bethought itself' or 'willed'—thus disregarding the marked visual component in this verb. The renderings 'visualised' or even 'imagined' reflect more adequately the intention of the original
28. Plotinus, *Enneads* V.1.6 (E. O'Brien's transl.)
29. S. Radhakrishnan, *Indian Philosophy*, volume II, p. 261
30. See *Bṛhadāraṇyaka-Upaniṣad* V.5; also: *Chāndogya-Upaniṣad* VII.10.1
31. See *Chāndogya-Upaniṣad* I.9.1
32. S. N. Dasgupta, *A History of Indian Philosophy*, volume II, p. 465

33. R. C. Zaehner, *op.cit.*, p. 14
34. See, for example, *Muṇḍaka-Upaniṣad* I.1.7
35. These parallels were first pointed out by R. C. Zaehner, *Mysticism Sacred and Profane* (Oxford, 1957)
36. S. Radhakrishnan, *op.cit.*, volume II, p. 269
37. B. N. Seal, *The Positive Sciences of the Ancient Hindus* (London, 1915)
38. S. N. Dasgupta, *op. cit.*, volume I, pp. 251–2
39. For instance: A. A. Macdonell, *A History of Sanskrit Literature* (London, 1900), p. 386: 'Of the orthodox systems, by far the most important are the pantheistic Vedānta . . . and the atheistic Sānkhya, which, for the first time in the history of the world, asserted the complete independence of the human mind and attempted to solve its problems solely by the aid of reason.'
40. K. B. N. Rao, *Theism of Pre-Classical Sāṃkhya* (Prasaranga, 1966), p. 432
41. See, for example, *Mahābhārata* XII.300.7
42. S. Radhakrishnan, *The Brahma Sūtra*: *The Philosophy of Spiritual Life* (London, 1960), pp. 155–6
43. *Bṛhadāraṇyaka-Upaniṣad* IV.4.5
44. S. T. Coleridge, *Biographia Literaria*, volume I, p. 119; Quoted in S. Radhakrishnan, *The Brahma Sūtra*, p. 194, *fn.* 5
45. S. Radhakrishnan, *The Bhagavadgītā*, p. 49
46. See Manu's *Dharma-Śāstra* X.45
47. G. Heard, *Pain, Sex and Time*: *A New Hypothesis of Evolution* (London, 1939), p. 273
48. G. Heard, *op.cit.*, p. 274
49. See *Chāndogya-Upaniṣad* IV.4
50. *Dharma-Śāstra* X.65
51. *Mahābhārata* III.180.21
52. *Mahābhārata* III.216.13
53. See *Bhagavad-Gītā* IX.32
54. *Mahābhārata* XII.232.14–17 (Sukthankar's ed.)
55. *Mahābhārata* XII.246.9–10[a] (Sukthankar's ed.)
56. See *Bhagavad-Gītā* XVIII.30–2
57. *Mahābhārata* XII.242.3–4[a]
58. S. Radhakrishnan, *The Bhagavadgītā*, p. 51
59. See G. Feuerstein & J. Miller, *A Reappraisal of Yoga*, pp. 3ff
60. See K. N. Upadhyaya, *Early Buddhism and the Bhagavadgītā*, pp. 477–8
61. *Viveka-Cūḍāmaṇi*, verse 11
62. *Viveka-Cūḍāmaṇi*, verse 56
63. *Yoga-Bhāṣya* I.12
64. See *Yoga-Sūtra* II.31
65. See *Bhagavad-Gītā* XVI.1–3, etc

66. Quoted in J. Gebser, 'Asien und die Wissenschaft des Abendlandes', off-print from *Indo-Asia*, part II (1962)
67. The evolution of ethical thought in India has been admirably delineated in its various phases by P. V. Kane, *History of Dharmaśāstra*, 5 volumes
68. S. Radhakrishnan, *The Bhagavadgītā*, p. 47
69. See E. Conze, *Buddhist Thought in India* (London, 1962), pp. 92–106
70. The translation is Zaehner's
71. G. Feuerstein & J. Miller, *A Reappraisal of Yoga*, p. 138
72. This is the archaic identity of microcosm and macrocosm transposed on to the ethical level
73. S. N. Dasgupta, *op.cit.*, volume II, p. 486
74. See R. C. Zaehner, *Mysticism Sacred and Profane* (Oxford, 1957)
75. R. C. Zaehner translates the compound *brahma-nirvāṇa* with 'Nirvāna that is Brahman too', but this is rather awkward.
76. See S. Radhakrishnan, *Indian Philosophy*, volume I, p. 578
77. See *Bhagavad-Gītā* XII.5
78. Meister Eckehart, Sermon 45 (Quint's ed.)
79. Meister Eckehart, Sermon 28 (Quint's ed.)

APPENDIX I
THE CONVERSATION BETWEEN AṢṬĀVAKRA AND VANDIN

Vandin said:

A single fire flames forth as many [sparks]. The one sun illuminates this entire [world]. One hero, the king-of-celestials [i.e. Indra], slays the enemy-forces. And the one Yama is the lord of [all] the fore-fathers. (8)

Aṣṭāvakra said:

The two friends Indra and Agni roam [ever together]. [There are] two divine seers: Nārada and Parvata. [There are] two Aśvins. Also, a chariot has two wheels. Husband and wife procure [offspring] as a couple [as ordained by] the creator. (9)

Vandin said:

Three [kinds of] birth are produced by [one's] acts. Three [priests] together perform the *vājapeya*-sacrifice. The priests perform [sacrifices] at three times [of the day]. [There are] three spheres, and three are said to be the *jyotīṛṣis*. (10)

Aṣṭāvakra said:

The life-station (*niketa*) of the *brāhmaṇas* is of four kinds. The four castes (*varṇa*) perform the sacrifice. [There are] four regions (*diś*). Of four kinds is the racial-colour (*varṇa*). Also, as is continually reiterated, a cow has four legs. (11)

Vandin said:

[There are] five fires and five feet to the *paṅkti*-metre. [There are] five sacrifices, five senses. In the Veda five hair-locks of the *apsaras* are mentioned. And five sacred rivers are known in this world. (12)

Aṣṭāvakra said:

Six [cows] are said to be the fee for kindling [the sacrificial fire].

Also, six are the seasons of the wheel-of-time. [There are] six senses, and the six Pleiades (*kṛttikā*). Six *sādyaska*-sacrifices are known in all the Vedas. (13)

Vandin said:

[There are thought to be] seven [kinds of] domesticated animals, [and] seven wild animals. Seven metres are used in a sacrifice. [There are] seven seers and seven [forms of] honouring. And, as is known, the lute (*vīṇā*) has seven strings. (14)

Aṣṭāvakra said:

Eight *śāṇā*-measures make a hundred-weight. Also Śarabha, the [legendary] lion-slayer, has eight legs. We hear that there are eight Varsus among the deities. And the stake (*yūpa*) used in all sacrifices has eight angles. (15)

Vandin said:

Nine are said to be the fire-offerings to the fore-fathers. Also, it is said [that there are] nine functions in the process-of-creation. Nine letters make up [the foot of the] *bṛhatī*-metre. Nine is also ever the number of figures [used in mathematics]. (16)

Aṣṭāvakra said:

[There are] said to be ten regions in the world of man. Ten times hundred are considered to be a thousand. Moreover, pregnancy lasts ten months. [There are] ten [teachers of] the One [Reality], ten foes [thereof], ten [who] honour [It]. (17)

Vandin said:

[There are] eleven [kinds of] sacrificial animals. [Furthermore, there are] eleven [types of] sacrificial-stakes, eleven forms of life-bearers. The Rudras in Heaven among the gods are [also] said to be eleven. (18)

Aṣṭāvakra said:

The year is said to have twelve months. Twelve letters [make up] the foot of the *jagatī*-metre. It is thought that there are twelve minor sacrifices. The wise proclaim that there are twelve Ādityas. (19)

Vandin said:

The thirteenth lunar day is said to be auspicious. There are thirteen islands on earth, and . . . (20[a])

(Here Vandin's speech breaks down. Aṣṭāvakra supplies the latter half of the verse.)

Aṣṭāvakra said:

[There are] thirteen offerings [presided over] by the strong Keśin.
Thirteen are said to be devoured by the *aticchanda*-metres. (21[b])

The real meaning of this highly enigmatic dialogue may be gathered from Nīlakaṇṭha's commentary on the *Mahābhārata*. Availing himself of various philosophical systems to combat his opponent, Vandin opens the controversy (verse 8) by saying that the senses are ruled over by the single faculty of reason (*buddhi*). Aṣṭāvakra, a stout adherent of the philosophy of Advaita-Vedānta, encounters (verse 9) that there is a second faculty besides that of reason, namely consciousness. Both together are responsible for man's sense-activity. Vandin now argues (verse 10) that more important than reason or consciousness is the power of one's acts (*karman*). But Aṣṭāvakra points out (verse 11) that the spell of the acts is broken when the 'fourth', that is, the Self (*ātman*), becomes manifest.

Vandin now switches to a different problem (verse 12). He states that there are only five senses and five corresponding sense-objects. Again, Aṣṭāvakra refutes his opponent's view (verse 13) by saying that there is a sixth sense, the mind (*manas*). Vandin accepts this, yet insists (verse 14) that man's experiences depend not only on these six senses, but also on the higher faculty of *buddhi*. In answer, Aṣṭāvakra introduces (verse 15) an eighth faculty, that of the sense of egohood (*ahaṃkāra*), which is present in all one's experiences.

Vandin now brings forward (verse 16), as ninth principle, the Sāṃkhya doctrine of *prakṛti* as the ultimate matrix of all manifested things. Aṣṭāvakra, however, countermines this viewpoint (verse 17) by advancing the Advaita-Vedānta notion of the illusoriness (*māyā*) of *prakṛti*: Only the Supreme Self is real. By coming into contact with the ten instruments-of-knowledge, i.e. the five cognitive and the five conative senses, the Self brings forth the entire manifestation.

Vandin proceeds to identify (verse 18) this Supreme Self with the human psyche, saying that the Self is not really free from the fetters of happiness and sorrow caused by the eleven objects-of-sense. Aṣṭāvakra refutes this view (verse 19): Self and psyche are not identical. The Self is beyond the ken of the senses and the mind.

Hence it is undemonstrable, and the only access to it is by exercising the twelve virtues, like truthfulness, self-restraint, sense-control, etc. Vandin argues (verse 20[a]) that these twelve virtues are not enough in themselves; enlightenment also depends on suitable external conditions. This is strictly denied by Aṣṭāvakra (verse 21[b]) who concludes the controversy by stating that the Self, which is essentially free, omniscient and omnipresent, appears to be 'bound' due to its connection with the thirteen psychic 'organs', *viz* the ten senses, the mind, the I-maker and the wisdom-faculty. He repeats that these thirteen faculties can be surmounted by the twelve virtues which lead directly to emancipation, that is, the Self's realisation of its eternal freedom.

APPENDIX II: GOD–UNITY IN DIVERSITY

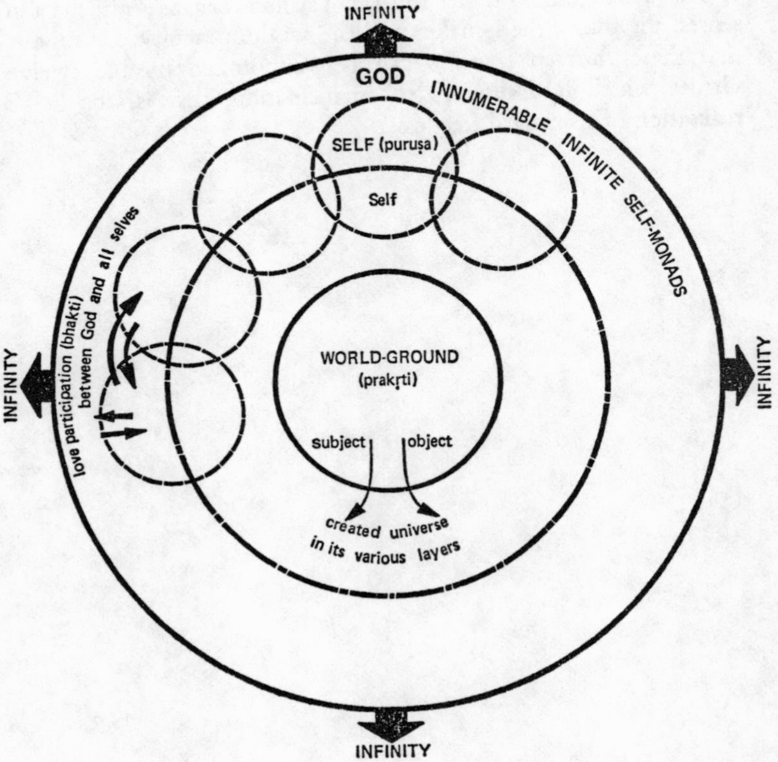

APPENDIX III: THE STRUCTURE OF THE WORLD

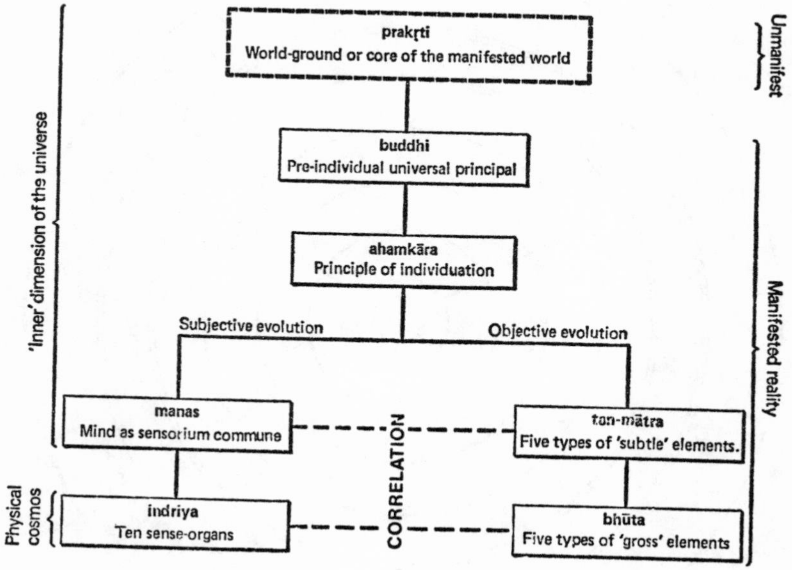

APPENDIX IV: THE STRATIFICATION OF INDIAN SOCIETY

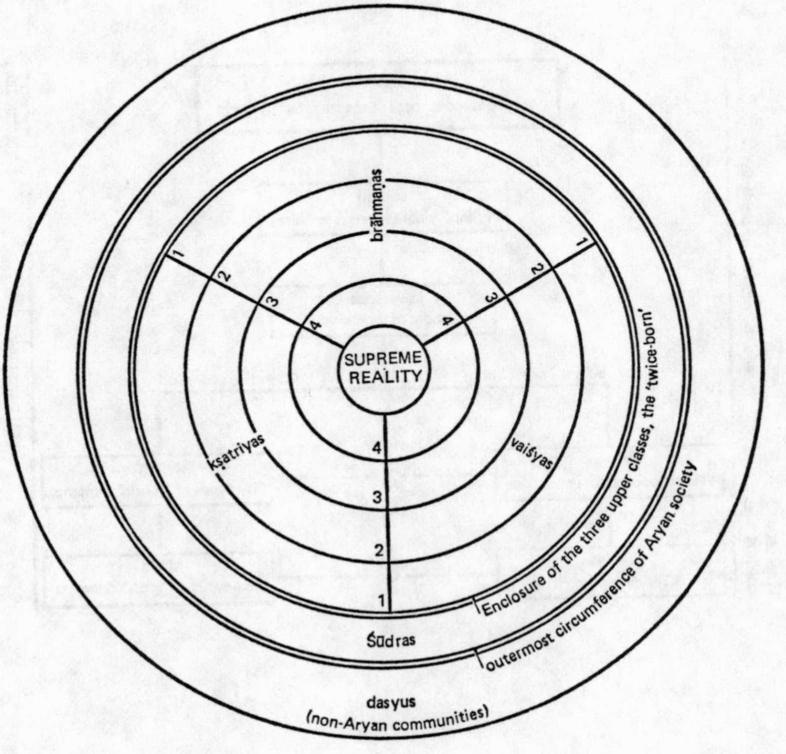

1 = pupilage *(brāhmacārya)*
2 = householder stage *(gṛhastha)*
3 = forest-dweller stage *(vānaprastha)*
4 = life stage of the renunciant *(saṃnyāsa)*

APPENDIX V: KṚṢṆA—TEACHER OF DHARMA

Kṛṣṇa appears in the *Mahābhārata* and the *Gītā* as a teacher of true *dharma*. Yet several interpreters have cast suspicion on his moral integrity. Noteworthy are the eloquent accusations of the archvillain Duryodhana in the epic itself. Are these charges justified?

Kṛṣṇa is a truly complex figure in the great epic story, and there are in fact many instances which seemingly reinforce this censorious attitude. Two main arguments are commonly put forward in Kṛṣṇa's defence. The first is that the Kṛṣṇa of the epic is different from the divine teacher of the *Gītā*. This view is absolutely unsound. As we have seen in the Introduction to this book, there is sufficient evidence to maintain that the *Gītā* is an integral part of the *Mahābhārata*, and therefore there is only one Kṛṣṇa, the incarnate God. The second 'excuse' for the imputed immorality of the greatest teacher of ethics is that Kṛṣṇa as a divine being is not subject to human laws. This is equally fallacious. Where, then, lies the truth?

It appears that the critics of Kṛṣṇa have failed to grasp the essential principle of his ethical teachings, namely that the supremacy of the moral order (*dharma*) must be safeguarded against *adharma* by any means. This, of course, does not imply the disreputable ethical maxim that the end justifies the means. Kṛṣṇa's transgressions of the existing moral code must be considered from a deeper point of view. His often unorthodox behaviour is not arbitrary. He tries to set an example of what it means to uphold the true *dharma*: the spirit of *dharma* must override the letter. Kṛṣṇa fights *adharma*, but at the same time he reprimands those who, like Yudhiṣṭhira the paragon of virtue in the epic, have a too narrow and formal conception of *dharma*. He asks us not to be reluctant to fight *adharma* with its own means, if thereby we can help to re-establish the lost order. Perfect *dharma* is hardly possible in real life. Therefore we should not be afraid of fighting greater evil by lesser wrong where the preservation of *dharma* is at stake. This is the great lesson which pacifists have to learn.

SELECT BIBLIOGRAPHY

[Śrī] Aurobindo. *Essays on the Gita* (New York, Sri Aurobindo Library, 1950)

——*On Yoga* (Pondicherry, Sri Aurobindo Ashram, 1958)

Bahm, A. J. *The Bhagavad Gita or The Wisdom of Krishna* (Bombay, Somaiya Publications, 1970)

Bhattarcharji, S. *The Indian Theogony* (Cambridge, University Press, 1970)

Bhikshu Sangharakshita. *The Three Jewels: An Introduction to Buddhism* (London, Rider, 1967)

——*A Survey of Buddhism* (Bangalore, Indian Institute of World Culture, 1966[3])

Bleeker, C. J. and Widengreen, G. (eds.). *Historia Religionum: Handbook for the History of Religions* (Leiden, Brill, 1969–71), 2 volumes

Buitenen, J. A. B. van. *Rāmānuja on the Bhagavadgītā* (Delhi, Barnarsidass, repr. 1968)

Conze, E. *Buddhist Thought in India* (London, Allen & Unwin, 1962)

Conze, R. *et al.* (eds.). *Buddhist Texts Through the Ages* (New York, Harper & Row, 1964).

Daniélou, A. *Hindu Polytheism* (London, Routledge, 1964)

Dasgupta, S. N. *A History of Indian Philosophy* (Cambridge, University Press, 1922–55), 5 volumes

——*Hindu Mysticism* (Chicago, Open Court Publishing Co., 1927)

Date, V. H. *Brahma-Yoga of the Gītā* (New Delhi, Manoharlal, 1971)

Deutsch, E. and Buitenen, J. A. B. van (eds.). *A Source Book of Advaita-Vedānta* (Honolulu, University Press, 1971).

Divanji, P. C. *Critical Word-Index to the Bhagavadgītā* (Bombay, New Book Co., 1946)

Dürckheim, K. Graf von. *The Way of Transformation: Daily Life as Spiritual Exercise* (London, Allen & Unwin, 1971)

Edgerton, F. *The Beginnings of Indian Philosophy* (Cambridge, Harvard University Press, 1965)

——*The Bhagavad Gita* (Chicago and London, Open Court Publishing Co., 1925)

Eliade, M. *Images and Symbols: Studies in Religious Symbolism* (London, Harvill Press, 1961[2])

——*Yoga: Immortality and Freedom* (London, Routledge, 1958

Eliade, M. and Kitagawa, J. M. (eds.). *The History of Religions: Essays in Methodology* (Chicago, University Press, 1962)

Gauchhwal, B. S. *The Concept of Perfection in the Teachings of Kant and the Gītā* (Delhi, Banarsidass, 1967)

Gebser, J. *Ursprung und Gegenwart* (Stuttgart, Deutsche Verlagsanstalt, 1966²), 2 volumes

——*Asien lächelt anders* (Berlin, Ullstein, 1968)

Geldner, K. F. *Der Rigveda*, Harvard Oriental Series, volumes 33–6 (Cambridge, Harvard University Press, 1941–57)

Gonda, J. *Die Religionen Indiens*, Die Religionen der Menschheit, volumes 11 and 12 (Stuttgart, Kohlhammer, 1960 and 1963)

——*Viṣṇuism and Śivaism: A Comparison* (London, Athlone Press, 1970)

Guenther, H. V. *Buddhist Philosophy in Theory and Practice*, Pelican Original (Harmondsworth, Penguin Books, 1972)

Hill, W. D. P. *The Bhagavadgītā* (London, Oxford University Press, 1928)

Hopkins, E. W. *Ethics of India* (New Haven, Yale University Press, 1924)

Hospers, J. *Human Conduct: An Introduction to the Problems of Ethics* (New York and Harcourt, Brace & World Inc., 1961)

Hume, R. E. *The Thirteen Principal Upanishads* (London, Oxford University Press, 1958⁴)

Kane, P. V. *History of Dharmaśāstra* (Poona, Bhandarkar Oriental Institute, 1930–53), 4 volumes

Khair, G. S. *Quest for the Original Gita* (Bombay, Somaiya Publications, 1969)

Koelman, G. M. *Pātañjala Yoga* (Poona, Papal Athenaeum, 1970)

Krishna Prem. *The Yoga of the Bhagavat Gita* (London, Watkins, 1969)

Larson, G. J. *Classical Sāṃkhya* (Delhi, Barnarsidass, 1969)

MacIntyre, A. *A Short History of Ethics* (London, Routledge, 1968²)

Mahādeva Śāstri, A. *The Bhagavad-Gītā, With the Commentary of Śrī Śankarachāryā* (Madras, R. Sastrulu, 1961⁵)

Mehta, R. *From Mind to Supermind* (Bombay, Manaktalas, 1966)

Mishra, U. *A Critical Study of the Bhagavadgītā* (Allahabad, Tirabhukti Publications, 1954)

Murti, T. R. V. *The Central Philosophy of Buddhism* (London, Allen & Unwin, 1960)

Nataraja Guru. *The Bhagavad Gita* (London, Asia Publishing House, 1961)

Paradkar, M. D. (ed.). *Studies in the Gita* (Bombay, Popular Prakashan, 1970)

Parrinder, G. *Upanishads, Gītā and Bible* (New York, Association Press, 1962)

——*Avatar and Incarnation* (London, Faber, 1970)

Radhakrishnan, S. *The Bhagavadgītā* (London, Allen & Unwin, 1960⁶)

——*Indian Philosophy* (London, Allen & Unwin, repr. 1951), 2 volumes

Radhakrishnan, S. and Raju, P. T. (eds.). *The Concept of Man: A Study in Comparative Philosophy* (London, Allen & Unwin, 1966²)

Rau, S. S. *Bhagavad-Gita* (Madras, Natesan, 1906)

Ray, P. C. *The Mahābhārata* (Calcutta, Bharata Press, 1884 ff.), 14 volumes

Roy, S. C. *The Bhagavad-Gita and Modern Scholarship* (London, Luzac, 1941)

Seeger, E. *The Five Sons of King Pandu* (London, Dent, 1970)

Sharma, C. *A Critical Survey of Indian Philosophy* (London, Rider, 1960)

Singer, M. (ed.). *Krishna: Myths, Rites and Attitudes*, Phoenix Book (Chicago, University Press, 1968)

Sukthankar, V. S. *On the Meaning of the Mahābhārata* (Bombay, Asiatic Society, 1957)

Telang, K. T. *Bhagavadgītā with the Sanatsujātīya and the Anugītā*, Sacred Books of the East, volume 8 (Oxford, Clarendon Press, 1908²)

Thapar, R. *A History of India*, Pelican Original, volume 1 (Harmondsworth, Penguin Books, 1966)

Upadhyaya, K. N. *Early Buddhism and the Bhagavadgītā* (Delhi, Banarsidass, 1971)

Vadekar, D. D. *Bhagavad-Gita: A Fresh Study* (Poona, Oriental Book Agency, 1928)

Vora, D. P. *Evolution of Morals in the Epics* (Bombay, Popular Book Depot, 1959)

Warnock, M. *Ethics since 1900* (London, Oxford University Press, 1966²)

Whitney, W. D. *Atharva-Veda Saṃhitā*, Harvard Oriental Series, volumes 7 and 8 (Cambridge, Harvard University Press, 1905)

Zaehner, R. C. *Concordant Discord* (Oxford, Clarendon Press, 1970)

——*The Bhagavad-Gītā* (Oxford, Clarendon Press, 1969)

INDEX

Parapsychology, 129
parā-prakṛti (higher nature of God), 88
Parāsara, 42
Pascal, B., 112
Patañjali, 29, 87, 91, 140, 144
phala (fruit), 156ff.
Phenomenology, 86
Philosophy,
nature of, 79, 87
East and West, 94
physis, 101
pitṛ-loka (abode of ancestors), 47
Plato, 72
Plotinus, 95, 100, 106
pluralism,
of Theravāda, 85
Polytheism, 72
Prajāpati, 64
prakṛti (world-ground), 88, 89, 93, 101ff., see also Nature
pralaya (absorption of creation), 104
prāṇa (vital force), 143
praṇava (syllable *oṃ*), 25
prāṇāyāma (control of vital force), 143, 144
prasāda, see grace
prema (love), 33
priesthood, 23, 24, 98
Protagoras, 72
Psychology, 131
Psychotherapy, 79, 128
Purāṇas, 36, 85, 99
composed by Vyāsa, 40
pūrṇa, see Whole
pūrṇa-yoga (holistic Yoga), 132
puruṣa (Primeval Giant), 75, see also Self
puruṣa-artha (human goal), 121, 122
puruṣa-sūkta (hymn of man), 75
puruṣottama (supreme Man), 71, 85, 92
Pythagoras, 96

R

Radhakrishnan, S., 20, 34, 44, 56, 101, 107, 115, 126, 161
rājanya (warrior), 116ff.
rajas (dynamic principle), 54, 103, 112, 126, 156, see also *guṇa*
Rāma, 46
Rāmānanda, 32
Ramana Maharshi, 134
Rāmānuja, 31, 32, 93, 139
Rāmāyaṇa, 46
Rao, K. B., 110
Rāvaṇa, 46
reincarnation, 114, see also *karman*
religion, 72, 119, 149
renunciant (*saṃnyāsin*), 120, 121
renunciation (saṃnyāsa), 132ff.,
absent in Vedic age, 22
dangers of, 30
in action, 56, 133
Ṛgveda, 21, 98, 100, 116, 129, see also *Vedas*
ṛṣi (seer), 20, 98
ṛta (cosmic order), 22, 23, 126, 154, 158

S

sacrifice (*yajña*), 23, 24, 56, 64
archetypal, 65, 75
sādhāraṇa-dharma (common moral code), 118
Saher, P. J., 15
Śaiva-Siddhānta, 14
Śaivism, 76
sākṣin (witness), 90, see also Self
śakti (power), 101
Śaktivāda, 14
Śakuni, 52
Śalya, 48
śama (quiescence), 139
samādhi (enstasy), 144